兵法

孫子

THE
ART
OF
STRATEGY

THE
ART
OF
STRATEGY

A New Translation of Sun Tzu's Classic
The Art of War

R.L. WING

BROADWAY BOOKS / NEW YORK

BROADWAY

A hardcover edition of this book was originally published in 1988 by Doubleday. It is here reprinted by arrangement with Doubleday.

Broadway Books titles may be purchased for business or promotional use or for special sales. For information, please write to: Special Markets Department, Random House, Inc., 1540 Broadway, New York, NY 10036.

BROADWAY BOOKS and its logo, a letter B bisected on the diagonal, are trademarks of Broadway Books, a division of Random House, Inc.

Visit our website at www.broadwaybooks.com

First Broadway Books trade paperback edition published 2000.

DESIGN: *Rita Aero*
RESEARCH: *Jacqueline Tsang, Chi Yuen Tsang, Fred Cline*
CALLIGRAPHY: *Tse Leong Toy*
COVER CALLIGRAPHY: *Lam-po Leong*
EDITORIAL CONSULTING: *Richard Rosenberg, James Webb*

The Library of Congress has catalogued the paperback edition as:
Sun-tzu, 6th cent. B.C.
   The art of strategy.
   "A Dolphin Book"
   1. Military art and science—Early works to 1800.
I. Wing, R. L.   II. Title.
U101.S95   1988   355'.02   87-37465
ISBN 0-385-23784-7

23 22 21 20 19 18

CONTENTS

NOTES ON THE TRANSLATION   10

SUN TZU   12

THE ART OF STRATEGY   14

Chapter One — THE CALCULATIONS   17
    (Analyzing the Conflict)

  1.   The Five Fundamentals of Strategy
  2.   Examining the Fundamentals
  3.   The Tao of Paradox
  4.   Foretelling Triumph

Chapter Two — THE CHALLENGE   29
    (Estimating the Costs)

  5.   Knowing the Costs
  6.   Swift Strategies
  7.   Using the Opponent's Resources
  8.   Incorporating the Opponent's Strength

Chapter Three — THE PLAN OF ATTACK   41
    (Developing an Error-Free Strategy)

  9.   Engaging the Entire System
10.   The Rule of Numbers
11.   Three Errors of Leaders
12.   The Essentials of Triumph

Chapter Four — POSITIONING 53
(Positioning Yourself for Triumph)

13. The Power Defense
14. The Triumph of No Effort
15. The Position of No Error
16. The Five Strategic Arts

Chapter Five — DIRECTING 65
(Positioning Your Opponent for Defeat)

17. The Positioned Strategy
18. The Power of Surprise
19. Moving the Opponent About
20. Using Others to Create Momentum

Chapter Six — ILLUSION AND REALITY 77
(Using Camouflage)

21. Creating Imbalance
22. Distorting the Opponent's Position
23. Adjusting the Opponent's Numbers
24. Reacting with Systematic Positioning

Chapter Seven — ENGAGING THE FORCE 89
(Maneuvering for Advantage)

25. Direct and Indirect Tactics
26. Avoiding Competition
27. Flexibility and Imitation
28. Controlling the Variations

Chapter Eight — THE NINE VARIATIONS 101
(Spontaneity in the Field)

29. Situational Strategies
30. Combining Advantages and Disadvantages
31. Anticipating the Opponent
32. Five Weaknesses in Leaders

Chapter Nine — MOVING THE FORCE   113
(Confrontation in the Field)

33. Using the Situation
34. Determining the Opponent's Strategy
35. Determining the Opponent's Vulnerability
36. The Cultivation of Allegiance

Chapter Ten — SITUATIONAL POSITIONING   125
(Positioning During Confrontation)

37. The Six Positions
38. The Six Strategic Mistakes
39. Superior Leadership
40. Knowing the Situation

Chapter Eleven — THE NINE SITUATIONS   137
(Mobilizing During Confrontation)

41. Situational Response
42. The Spirit of the Corps
43. The Way of the Adventurer
44. The Strategy of the Superior Leader

Chapter Twelve — THE FIERY ATTACK   149
(The Decisive Thrust)

45. The Five Fiery Attacks
46. The Five Fiery Variations
47. The Decisive Techniques
48. The Ultimate Restraint

Chapter Thirteen — THE USE OF INTELLIGENCE   161
(The Information Advantage)

49. Obtaining Foreknowledge
50. The Divine Web
51. The Importance of Counterintelligence
52. The Essence of Strategy

NOTES ON THE TRANSLATION

The Chinese classics were written in a very general universal style. They were meant to be templates for life experiences — templates to be used by anyone, at any time, in any situation. The written language of China lends itself well to this phenomenon. Each character, or ideogram, is a multi-dimensional picture of an idea. Each can be looked at from a number of angles and experienced in a variety of ways. This mutable quality in the written language somehow triggers responses that feel personal and timely. For this reason, books like the *I Ching* (*The Book of Change*), the *Tao Te Ching* (*The Tao of Power*), or *The Art of Strategy* seem to have as many meanings as there are individuals experiencing them. They have retained their startling relevance through the centuries and are meaningful to every variety of human experience. In a word, they are immortal.

Reading a philosophical work like *The Art of Strategy* in Chinese is an elegant experience. There is a harmony and resolution to each phrase, much as in a piece of music. The Chinese classics were frequently written with a simple rhythmic balance so that the words would be easy to remember — after all, there was no printing technology, nor was there paper (books were inscribed on bamboo strips).

The rhythmic, economic style of *The Art of Strategy* translates well into English. The structure of the text in this book represents, very nearly, the word-by-word meter of the original. The Chinese script also appears, and the directness of this translation should allow those so inclined to follow along — even without prior knowledge of the characters. Just keep in mind that the Chinese type runs in vertical columns read top to bottom and right to left.

I have attempted to follow the original script word for word, and to remain vigilant against the introduction of "helpful" terminology. As much as possible, the characters have been translated consistently throughout, while the words chosen are very general ones, so that any nuance in meaning may be added by the reader. Where I have unable or unwilling to translate directly, I have footnoted so in the text.

I have translated the character *bing* as "strategy" both in the title and throughout the text. This is a common translation of *bing*, but the reader should note that the word has also been translated as "war," "military," "tactic," "combat," "battle," "maneuver," "weapon," "conflict," and so forth. I have chosen "strategy" because I believe that it is most faithful to Sun Tzu's intended objective: the achievement of triumph through tactical positioning, without resorting to battle.

The only character I have left untranslated is Tao. In one or two instances, when it was critical to the meaning of the sentence, Tao was translated as "way." Tao comes from Taoism, which was the prevailing philosophy at the time *The Art of Strategy* was written. Curiously, in all but one translation of Sun Tzu's work, Tao has been translated in a rough, utilitarian way as a noun or verb suggesting mobilization, which has the unfortunate effect of stripping the significant philosophical context out of *The Art of Strategy*. Tao is a very difficult word to translate, but it can be paraphrased as "the smooth way that things tend to operate in nature." When events are manipulated, they are not Tao, and outcomes are dangerously uncontrolled. To have the Tao at work in a situation or a strategy is considered the greatest of advantages, since the operation becomes effortless and the results predictable. It is as though all the forces of nature are working toward one's own objective.

The Art of Strategy has been widely translated, and the translations generally reflect the cultural or religious background of the translators. Since the time of the Tang Dynasty (A.D. 618 to 906) continuing through to the present, Sun Tzu's work was known and studied in Japan. It was not introduced into the West until 1772 when the French Jesuit Fr. P. Amiot translated it from Chinese into French. It has been said that this version was a favorite of Napoleon. Translations of Sun Tzu began to appear in Russia as early as the 1800s, the most notable a 1950 translation by N. Konrad.

In 1905, British Army Capt. E. F. Calthrop translated *The Art of Strategy* into English from a Japanese translation. It was soon after translated directly from Chinese into English by Lionel Giles, curator of Oriental books and manuscripts at the British Museum. The Giles translation, entitled *The Art of War*, was published in 1910 and has remained in print ever since, most recently reissued in a 1983 edition with commentary by American author James Clavell. In 1910 the book was translated into German by von Bruno Navarra, while in 1956 the Soviet military published a Chinese-to-Russian translation by Lt. J. I. Siderenko. An American translation by retired U. S. Marine Brig. Gen. Samuel B. Griffith, entitled *The Art of War*, was published in 1963. This version is currently available as are two English translations by Chinese scholars: *The Art of War* by Cheng Lin and *Principles of Conflict* by Tang Zi-Chang.

Many commentaries and annotations of *The Art of Strategy* have been composed over the centuries, but Sun Tzu himself wrote only thirteen chapters. In fact, the book is sometimes called *Sun Tzu's Thirteen Chapters*. I have broken each of the thirteen, at appropriate intervals, into four parts, which has resulted in fifty-two separate passages. The thirteen chapter titles are Sun Tzu's, but the titles of the individual passages are my own. They are there merely to suggest the specific subject of each. The subtitles (in parentheses) that appear in the thirteen chapter introductions help describe the topic covered in that chapter, and are also mine. The dates used in this translation are from Joseph Needham's *Science and Civilisation in China*. The English spellings of Chinese words are from the Wade-Giles system.

BING, THE IDEOGRAM FOR "STRATEGY"

— R. L. Wing

SUN TZU

More than twenty-three centuries have passed since Sun Tzu wrote *The Art of Strategy*, one of the world's earliest, and certainly its most unusual, military treatise. In his fifty-six-hundred-word classic, Sun Tzu put forth a tightly compressed set of principles for achieving triumph over opposition. What is most remarkable about his book is its central premise: A true victory can be won only with a strategy of tactical positioning, so that the moment of triumph is effortless and destructive conflict is averted. Sun Tzu pointed out: "Those who win one hundred triumphs in one hundred conflicts do not have supreme skill. Those who have supreme skill use Strategy to bend others without coming to conflict."

There has been some controversy over if and when Sun Tzu existed, but modern scholarship suggests that the *The Art of Strategy* was indeed written by a single author, probably Sun Tzu, and it is now generally believed to have been written sometime just before or during the Warring States period (480 to 221 B.C.). Around that time, Gautama, Buddhah was on his pilgrimage through India; Zoroaster was in Persia (Iran) preparing the philosophical ground from which Islamic thought would bloom; the Torah had just become the moral essence of the Jewish state; Socrates, Plato, and Aristotle were in Greece developing what was to become Western philosophy; and Lao Tzu and Confucius were nearby, cultivating their own ideas. Meanwhile, Alexander the Great was gathering an army that would successfully conquer India, Persia, and Greece. It was a significant moment in human history, rich with new ideas and fierce aggression.

The Warring States period of Sun Tzu's time is aptly named. During this era, more than three hundred wars were fought between the separate states of China and against the ruling dynasty, the Chou. To make a twentieth-century analogy, the Chinese of the Warring States experienced World War II continually for 150 years. Of course, the weapons were quite different, but the armies were nearly as large and the devastation and human suffering just as profound. Today, the chariots and crossbows are gone, but the conflict, throughout the world, is exactly the same: a struggle for ideological supremacy and the control of resources.

The China of 300 B.C. presents an interesting microcosm of the world today. For the Chinese, their separate states in conflict was the world at war — to them, China was the entire world. Each individual state had a burning quest, if not for dominance, at least for survival. Surrounded by the devastation of his war-torn world, Sun Tzu achieved a basic awareness that is only now reaching the twentieth-century mind: It is not individually but altogether, as a single and complete entity, that the people of the world face survival or extinction. Using this philosophy, Sun Tzu developed his treatise *The Art of Strategy*, outlining specific strategies to overcome conflicts while viewing the world as a complete and interdependent system that must be preserved. To employ this premise, no one part of the system can triumph if it destroys another part, for this will damage everyone. In essence, Sun Tzu described a social strategy for overcoming conflicts that works very much the way the body's immune system works: It is designed to fight off invaders, suppress insurgency, overwhelm malignancies, and remove hostile agents — all without damaging the supporting system.

Sun Tzu succeeded in writing one of the most widely translated and thoroughly read books in the world today. His strategy is based on the laws of nature — both human nature and nature at large. Since all of life is subject to these laws, whether they are enacted microscopically or sociologically, Sun Tzu's treatise is an universal template that shows the way to triumph over life's conflicts — from the interpersonal to the international. The tactics presented in *The Art of Strategy* are powerful tools that can be used to overcome psychological obstacles, environmental discord, personal opposition, and organizational contention. The strategy follows a direct path that escalates until victory is assured. From analysis and projection, through planning and positioning, and on to confrontation, Sun Tzu explains such techniques as the use of camouflage, the creation of illusion, and the gathering of intelligence. Individuals who are ready to overcome their problems once and for all and assume control of their own destiny will find in this book what Sun Tzu concluded was "The Essence of Strategy."

SUN TZU

THE ART OF STRATEGY

The Art of Strategy presents a humane and intelligent method for triumph over nonnegotiable conflicts. Nonnegotiable conflicts are obstacles that stand in the way of meaningful growth in life. We can be blocked by obstacles in our personalities, in our surroundings, or in our interpersonal relationships. As these obstacles become clear to us, we experience an inner crisis, because we recognize this threat to our personal fulfillment and happiness. At this point, we make a choice: We either learn to live with the conflict by limiting our options and compromising our goals; or we remove the conflict by positioning it elsewhere or neutralizing its impact in our lives.

The Art of Strategy is designed for those who decide to push their conflicts out of their lives. It is for individuals who view the world as a place full of interesting options, and who plan to fully explore their potential. When confronted with an obstacle — a crippling character flaw, an unfulfilling occupation, or a debilitating interpersonal relationship — they develop a strategy to overcome that conflict and emerge victorious from its influence. They refuse to compromise their hopes or limit their opportunities. A game of chess cannot be resolved through compromise — nor can poor health, or a demeaning career, or a destructive relationship. These are life-damaging situations that must be and can be unconditionally overcome. To achieve this aim, four types of conflict to which Sun Tzu's strategies can be effectively applied are presented in the book:

CONFLICT IN THE SELF   In an inner conflict, a part of your self is interfering with positive growth in your life. You must not underestimate this inner opponent, for it can be as powerful as that part of your self that desires change. It draws on the same strengths and is aware of the same weaknesses. To overwhelm your inner opponent — whether it is a habit that should be broken or a psychological barrier that must be overcome — you must develop a strategy that will refocus your energies and restructure your personality. As difficult as this sounds, it is the key to a certain and lasting triumph.

CONFLICT IN THE ENVIRONMENT   In an environmental conflict, your surroundings — at home or at work, logistically or politically, are limiting your personal growth or compromising your principles. Many of your decisions, actions, and associations have kept you in your environment — were that not so, you would be elsewhere. Through your participation, you are supporting the very structure you wish to alter or transcend. Consequently, real and lasting solutions require exceptional and subtle strategies. Environmental conflicts are overcome only by re-forming your relationship to the environment and assuming more control, or by detaching yourself from the environment and leaving it behind.

CONFLICT WITH ANOTHER   In an interpersonal conflict, your opponent is not an individual, but a relationship that is negatively affecting your life. Interpersonal problems occur in business, in the family, and in love relationships, and most can be resolved through simple negotiations. However, when an interpersonal conflict blocks your development or happiness, the relationship can rarely be salvaged. These are conflicts that repeat again and again because the basic interaction is unbalanced and unloving. Once you have identified a deep, unresolvable interpersonal conflict, strong determination and a clear strategy are required. Generally, your triumph over an interpersonal conflict will completely alter or end the relationship.

CONFLICT AMONG LEADERS   Interorganizational conflicts arise out of disagreements over ideologies or resources, and can occur among social groups, in business, and in politics. Conflicts among leaders are a significant challenge because the fates of so many others are affected by the outcome. Therefore, a careful, prudent strategy must be employed, one that leads to triumph while protecting everyone concerned. When such a challenge is undertaken, the ideal strategy is to subdue the opposing organization through tactical positioning — well in advance of confrontation — so that your triumph is obvious and inevitable and both organizations are preserved. This is the ultimate challenge in *The Art of Strategy*.

Sun Tzu's classic text can be read in an afternoon, but it can take a year or more to learn how to spontaneously employ its strategies in everyday conflicts. A one-year calendar/workbook has been interspersed into the passages of this book, to be used by those who would like to learn *The Art of Strategy* systematically, and integrate into their lives its tactics for averting conflict or winning in confrontation. To the Chinese, the cycle of four seasons represented a complete period of experience, beginning with the spring of new growth, the summer of work, the autumn of harvest, and the winter of rest. To mark a lasting change — whether a change in habit, environment, relationship, or government — a full year must pass; the four seasons must cycle.

Each of the fifty-two passages represents a week-long thought-experiment in strategy. Each has notations for seven days, and note space to describe progress or insights. To learn *The Art of Strategy*, begin at any time, but begin at the beginning. Fill in the days and dates, and use the calendar, as you normally would, for one year. Read and reflect on each passage for one full week. Remain aware of the conflicts in your life, and use the strategy as you are able. When a year has passed, read the book through one more time. Your conflicts will be behind you and *The Art of Strategy* will be yours.

1 year = 52 weeks

ARCHER ARMING
A CROSSBOW

CHAPTER ONE

THE
CALCULATIONS

(ANALYZING THE CONFLICT)

SUN TZU BELIEVED THAT EVEN BEFORE CONSIDERING A CON-frontation — for whatever purpose — it is essential to Calculate a complete analysis of the situation. The strengths and weaknesses of one's position, the relationship between one's goals and the goals of society at large, the intensity of one's courage and determination, and the worthiness and integrity of one's objective must all be carefully evaluated. He so thoroughly believed in the importance of a projective analysis that he said, "By observing only this, I can see triumph or defeat."

Sun Tzu described the use of tactical paradox as a winning strategy, one that is employed by skillful leaders to gain significant advantage. Tactical paradox is the ability to project to the opponent a contradictory view of one's position or plan. Sun Tzu believed that this is fundamental to a clever strategy. "When able, they appear unable," he said. "When close, they appear distant.... They attack when the opponent is unprepared and appear where least expected. This is the Strategist's way of triumph."

CONFLICT IN THE SELF   The very moment you recognize an inner conflict is the right moment to plan a challenge. Inner conflicts can be bad habits, blocks to learning, destructive desires or weaknesses, undisciplined or unfocused motivation, or a personality damaged in childhood, resulting in low self-esteem or self-loathing.

Is this the right time to confront your inner opponent? Examine every facet of the situation and your position in it. If your goal is worthwhile, if you can achieve it through reasonable means, if the effort required is in balance with other factors in your life, and if you are truly determined, then the time is right. Do not, however, confront an inner conflict if the answer to any of these conditions is no. The chances of triumph will be unlikely and failure will strengthen your inner opponent. Instead, wait and build your strength and determination.

If you do decide to confront your conflict, develop a strategy to trick your inner opponent out of your life. Plan ahead, using rewards, distractions, substitutions, and inconsistencies to keep yourself in control and your inner opponent off balance. Prepare to act on whims. Look for unexpected opportunities. Remember your objective.

CONFLICT IN THE ENVIRONMENT   Environmental conflicts can sometimes be the most difficult to see clearly, and yet they inevitably determine your opportunity for self-development. Environmental discord can be caused by obstructed or stifling careers, destructive or depressing surroundings at home, a neighborhood or city environment that assults the senses, an uncomfortably complex lifestyle, or an unprincipled social milieu. These conflicts have one factor in common: They damage the inner self, or spirit.

Often you will not recognize environmental conflicts because you are in the midst of them, busily trying to adapt. Generally, what you experience of your conflict are side effects: poor health, depression, feelings of frustration or hopelessness, severe stress, anxiety, or a strong attraction to mindless activities. Only with careful analysis can you trace these symptoms to their cause. If you are caught in an environmental conflict, it must be transcended before your personal growth can continue.

Calculate the difficulty of the challenge you face in overcoming your environmental obstacle. Do you have the courage and the strength to transcend your environment? Can you visualize a positive objective to move toward? If you decide to go ahead with your challenge, do not announce your intentions. Arrive at a plan and evaluate your determination, all the while projecting business as usual.

CONFLICT WITH ANOTHER   A conflict with another individual can be as difficult to overcome as it is easy to perceive. Interpersonal conflicts occur in career or partnership situations, in intimate relationships that are unstable, or in any situation where individuals come together to interact or compete.

Many conflicts can be resolved through careful negotiations and compromises from which both parties emerge satisified. Nonnegotiable conflicts, however, are not only a barrier to personal growth, they can disrupt the well-being of others and destabilize the environment. These conflicts must be confronted — but only after the situation and its outcome are analyzed. Triumph over an interpersonal problem generally means that the relationship will change completely.

Should you decide to go ahead with your challenge, develop an objective and formulate a strategy to permanently change the way the relationship works. When you focus on your own growth and fulfillment — with or without the relationship — a worthwhile objective will emerge. Until your strategy is set in motion, however, do not project what you are planning to your opponent. Sun Tzu said: "Those who strategize, use the Tao of Paradox... and use confusion to take control."

CONFLICT AMONG LEADERS   When an organization finds itself in conflict with another organization, it is the strategic skill of the leader that will determine the outcome of events. Organizational conflicts can and do occur in business, in the community, and in the political arena, but only unskilled leaders work out their conflicts in courtrooms and on battlefields. Brilliant strategists rarely go to battle or to court; they generally achieve their objectives through tactical positioning well in advance of any confrontation.

Leaders whose organization is in conflict with a rival organization may initiate a challenge if the essentials of triumph are in place: They must be certain that their objective is worthwhile; that it is aligned with the larger trends and interests in society; that it is supported by all members of the organization; and that it can be achieved without compromising the basic principles of the organization. Furthermore, skilled leaders rely on the power of surprise: They are certain to mislead their adversaries about their position and their plans.

When a decision is made to challenge another organization, superior leaders spend their time and effort beforehand, Calculating, estimating, analyzing, and positioning. Sun Tzu pointed out: "Much computation brings triumph. Little computation brings defeat. How much more so with no computation at all!"

孫子曰：

兵者國之大事，死生之地，存亡之道，不可不察也。

故經之以五事，校之以計，而索其情：

一曰道，二曰天，三曰地，四曰將，五曰法。

道者，令民與上同意也，故可與之死，可與之生，而不畏危也。

天者，陰，陽，寒，暑，時制也。

地者，遠，近，險，易，廣，狹，死，生也。

將者，智，信，仁，勇，嚴，也。

法者，曲制，官道，主用也。

凡此五者，將莫不聞，知之者勝，不知者不勝。

THE FIVE FUNDAMENTALS OF STRATEGY

Sun Tzu said:

Strategy is the great Work of the organization.
In Situations of life or death, it is the Tao of survival or extinction.
Its study cannot be neglected.

Therefore, Calculate a plan with Five Working Fundamentals,
And examine the condition of each.
The first is Tao.
The second is Nature.
The third is Situation.
The fourth is Leadership.
The fifth is Art.

The Tao inspires people to share in the same ideals and expectations.
Hence, because they share in life and share in death,
The people do not fear danger.

Nature is the dark or light, the cold or hot, and the Systems of time.

Situation is the distant or immediate, the obstructed or easy,
The broad or narrow, and the chances of life or death.

Leadership is intelligence, credibility, humanity, courage, and discipline.

The Art is a flexible System
Wherein the View and its officials employ the Tao.

Leaders should not be unfamiliar with these Five.
Those who understand them will triumph.
Those who do not understand them will be defeated.

The word *View* can also be translated as "master" or "sovereign," and refers to
the mind, vision, or principle behind events.
Modern Chinese sometimes use this ideogram to refer to Jesus.

故校之以計，而索其情。

曰：主孰有道？
將孰有能？
天地孰得？
法令孰行？
兵眾孰強？
士卒孰練？
賞罰孰明？

吾以此知勝負矣。

將聽吾計，用之必勝，留之。

將不聽吾計，用之必敗，去之。

EXAMINING THE FUNDAMENTALS

When Calculating the Fundamentals,
Examine each one carefully.

Tell me:
Which View possesses the Tao?
Which Leader possesses competence?
Which can affect Nature and the Situation?

Which Art inspires a following?
Which Strategy has numerous strengths?
Which corps is highly trained?
Which has enlightened rewards and penalties?

It is through these that I know triumph or defeat.

If leaders who heed my Calculations are employed,
They are certain to triumph.
Retain them.

If leaders who do not heed my Calculations are employed,
They are certain to be defeated.
Remove them.

The term *Nature* comes from the Chinese word *jen*, which can also be translated as "heaven."
It refers to the actions and realm of the physical laws.

The term *Situation* comes from the Chinese word *ti*, which is also translated as "earth," "region," or "place."
It refers to the terrain where the laws of nature are manifest.

計利以聽，乃爲之勢，以佐其外。

勢者，因利而制權也。

兵者，詭道也。

故能而示之不能，用而示之不用，近而示之遠，遠而示之近。

利而誘之，亂而取之。

實而備之，強而避之，怒而撓之，卑而驕之，佚而勞之，親而離之，

攻其無備，出其不意。

此兵家之勝，不可先傳也

THE TAO OF PARADOX

Heed me by Calculating the advantages
And reinforce them by Directing outwardly.

Those who Direct, follow the advantages and adjust their formula.
Those who Strategize, use the Tao of Paradox.

Thus, when able, they appear unable.
When employed, they appear useless.
When close, they appear distant.
When distant, they appear close.

They lure through advantages,
And take control through confusion.

When complete, they appear to prepare.
When forceful, they appear evasive.
When angry, they appear to submit.
When proud, they appear to be humble.
When comfortable, they appear to toil.
When attached, they appear separated.

They attack when the opponent is unprepared
And appear where least expected.

This is the Strategist's way of triumph.
It must not be discussed beforehand.

夫未戰而廟算勝者，
得算多也。

未戰而廟算不勝者，
得算少也。

多算勝，少算不勝，
而況於無算乎！

吾以此觀之，勝負見矣。

FORETELLING TRIUMPH

Those who triumph,
Compute at their headquarters
A great number of factors
Prior to a challenge.

Those who are defeated,
Compute at their headquarters
A small number of factors
Prior to a challenge.

Much computation brings triumph.
Little computation brings defeat.
How much more so with no computation at all!

By observing only this,
I can see triumph or defeat.

The term *headquarters* comes from the Chinese word *miao*, which can also be translated as "temple" or "imperial court," and refers to the central place of ruling.

CHAPTER TWO

THE
CHALLENGE

(ESTIMATING THE COSTS)

*I*T IS ENORMOUSLY EXPENSIVE TO INITIATE A CHALLENGE — whether in time, money, or emotional energy — and any certainty of success must come through a careful evaluation of the costs well in advance of confrontation. Only in this way is a superior leader assured that the available resources will be adequate to sustain the effort through to triumph. To ensure that their support and strength are not compromised during conflict, skillful leaders are careful to plan a swift and timely strategy. Sun Tzu believed that a leader who initiated a lengthy operation would be defeated, and pointed out that "among strategies, therefore, the best triumph is a swift one.... A prolonged strategy has yet to bring advantage to an organization."

Sun Tzu also suggested that a vital tactic in any winning strategy includes the use of an adversary's resources. Enlightened strategists do not damage the support system or resources of their opponents. Instead, they make their opponents' strength work for them. In this way, their own powers are augmented and the entire System — of which everyone is a part — is not diminished.

CONFLICT IN THE SELF   The costs in overcoming inner conflicts are primarily emotional ones, and only through discipline and commitment can they be met. To emerge from this Challenge successfully, it is important to keep in mind that you are not attempting to destroy that part of yourself you wish to overcome. Instead, you are usurping its strengths so that you can put them to work in your new orientation.

When Challenging an inner opponent, avoid strategies that require long efforts through many stages of progress and plateau. Winning strategies are swift in their forward momentum, and they eliminate any possibility of retreat or regression. You cannot cross a wide river by returning periodically to the shore to rest. Halfway measures will merely compromise your strength, dilute your determination, and give your inner opponent the advantage.

If you decide that you can meet the emotional costs and do push away from the shore, look for ways to incorporate the considerable strength of the part of you that you have confronted. Try to harness your misdirected energies by viewing them in a positive, practical light. Plan to move forward swiftly without looking back.

CONFLICT IN THE ENVIRONMENT   Confronting an environmental conflict can be very expensive in time, money, and stress, but such a Challenge is necessary if personal growth is to continue. An environmental conflict may exist because a situation is inherently bad, or it may develop because your surroundings are not good for you at this time. You must either take control of your environment by assuming a more responsible role in it, or you must detach yourself from it altogether.

Because costs are so high and reversions or backsliding can be highly compromising to your strength, you must be certain that your resources have been carefully evaluated before engaging in this Challenge. If you determine that you must abandon your environment, plan a strategy that will take you to a place where you are able to support yourself independently. Considerable advance planning is essential to the success of this strategy.

To further ensure a successful transition, devise a way to "push against" your environment, thus utilizing its strength and rigidity to propel you forward. Do not build hesitation or dependence into your strategy; and be careful not to damage your environment in any way. You may very well need to use its resources later on.

CONFLICT WITH ANOTHER   The cost of an interpersonal Challenge is primarily an emotional one. Nonnegotiable conflicts can be very painful, since success generally comes through ending the relationship or changing it into a very different one. Therefore, careful evaluation and acceptance of the emotional costs of your Challenge are essential to your success.

Because of the intricacies and established patterns of interpersonal relationships, they are very difficult to Challenge. You must develop an all-encompassing strategy — one that can be implemented quickly and that provides a safe destination from which you will not be tempted to regress. Regression during an interpersonal confrontation will sap your strength and prolong your problems.

To help you develop a successful strategy for an interpersonal Challenge, evaluate and analyze the strengths and assets that have come from the relationship. Focus on these with an emotionally detached attitude, and use their energy — not to draw you back, but to help you visualize your way out of the cycle of conflict. Keep in mind that if you act in anger or with vengence, this positive energy will not be available to you.

CONFLICT AMONG LEADERS   Conflicts among leaders and between organizations are actually deeply rooted in the emotions, since our organizations define our growth as a culture as well as our possibilities for individual achievement. Before engaging in a Challenge, a leader must be certain that the organization is prepared to support the expense of a confrontation. A lack of resources will result in defeat during interorganizational confrontations.

In developing a strategy, unskilled leaders may make the error of believing that they can achieve a victory by destroying the resources of their opponents. Superior leaders know that any destruction damages the entire system, which in turn diminishes their own resources and opportunities. They never engage in destructive actions. Instead, through commerce, they concentrate on redirecting their opponent's resources to serve their own objectives.

A strategy that can be quickly mounted and swiftly executed is the key to triumph in interorganizational Challenges. Because of the vast expense and the large number of aligned minds necessary for support, prolonged strategies with periods of indecision or inaction are doomed to defeat. Sun Tzu pointed out that "crude yet quick Strategies have been known, but skill has yet to be observed in prolonged operations."

5
II

孫子曰：

凡用兵之法，馳車千駟，革車千乘，帶甲十萬，千里饋糧。

內外之費，賓客之用，膠漆之材，車甲之奉。

日費千金，然後十萬之師舉矣。

KNOWING THE COSTS

Sun Tzu said:

Generally, an Artful Strategy must be supported with
A thousand swift four-horse vehicles,
A thousand armored four-horse vehicles,
A hundred thousand armored troops,
And provisions transported for a thousand miles.

Moreover, further expenses must come from within
To be used for visitors and advisors;
Resin, varnish, and other construction materials;
And the maintenance of armor and vehicles.

To raise a corps of a hundred thousand,
A thousand pieces of gold will be spent each day.

The term *miles* comes from the Chinese word *li*, and actually refers to
a distance of about one third of a mile.

The term *vehicles* comes from an ideogram that is also translated as
"chariot," "wagon," or "cart."

其用戰也，勝。久則鈍兵挫銳，攻城則力屈，久暴師則國用不足。

夫鈍兵挫銳，屈力殫貨，則諸侯乘其弊而起，雖有智者。

不能善其後矣！

故兵聞拙速，未睹巧之久也。夫兵久而國利者，未之有也。

故不盡知用兵之害者，則不能盡知用兵之利也。

SWIFT STRATEGIES

Once a Challenge is executed, if triumph is prolonged,
The Strategy becomes dull and the vigor dampened.
If a Fortified Area is attacked,
One's strength is compromised.
If the Force's operations in the field are prolonged,
The support of the organization will be insufficient.

When Strategy is dull and vigor dampened,
When strength is compromised and resources depleted,
Other leaders will rise up
To seize the opportunity of this impairment.

Even those who are very clever
Cannot remedy the consequences!

Crude yet quick Stategies have been known,
But skill has yet to be observed in prolonged operations.
A prolonged Strategy has yet to bring advantage to an organization.

Therefore, those who are not entirely aware
Of Stategies that are disadvantageous,
Cannot be entirely aware
Of Stategies that are advantageous.

The term *Fortified Area* comes from a Chinese ideogram that refers to the walls of a city.
Large townships in early China were situated inside high walls built
to protect the town from bandits or invaders.

The term *Force* comes from an ideogram that can also be translated as
"military," "corps," or "national defense."

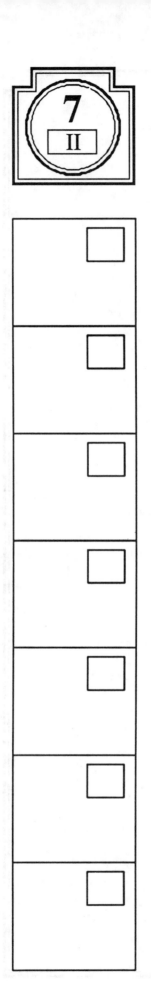

善用兵者，役不再籍，糧不三載。

取用於國，因糧於敵，故軍食可足也。

國之貧於師者遠輸，遠輸則百姓貧。

近於師者貴賣，貴賣則百姓財竭。

財竭則急於丘役，力屈財殫，中原內虛於家。

百姓之費，十去其七，公家之費。

破車罷馬，甲冑弓矢，戟楯蔽櫓，

丘牛大車，十去其六。

故智將務食於敵，食敵一鍾，當吾二十鍾；

萁秆一石，當吾二十石。

USING THE OPPONENT'S RESOURCES

Those who are skilled in executing a Strategy
Do not return again and again to levy taxes or to transport provisions.
They bring what is useful from the organization
And let their opponent show them the way to provisions.
In this way the Force is adequately fed.
When an organization transports to its corps at a distance,
The long-distance transport impoverishes the People.

When the corps is nearby, prices inflate;
And inflated prices use up the wealth of the People.
As the wealth is used up, taxes become larger and more urgent.
And as the state's wealth is depleted, its strength is compromised;
The homes of the People are emptied,
Along with seventy percent of their disposable income.

Sixty percent of the public expenditures go for
Broken vehicles and tired horses;
Armor, arrows, and crossbows;
Spears, shields, and mantelets;
And heavier oxen and larger vehicles.

Therefore, clever leaders endeavor to use their opponent's food.
One container of the opponent's food
Is the same as twenty containers of their own;
And one unit of fodder
Is the same as twenty units of their own.

The word *People* is from the Chinese expression "the hundred families," and refers to
the one hundred clan names — or to all of the population.

The word *unit* is from the Chinese word *tan*, which can also be translated as "picul":
a dry measure for grain that is roughly equal to 135 pounds.

The word *state* comes from the ideograms for "Central Plains,"
which refers to the downstream region of the Yellow River,
a heavily populated area in China then and now.

故殺敵者，怒也；取敵之利者，貨也。

故車戰，得車十乘以上，賞其先得者，而更其旌旗。車，雜而乘之·卒，善而養之。

是謂勝敵而益強。

故兵貴勝，不貴久。

故知兵之將，民之司命，國家安危之主也。

INCORPORATING THE OPPONENT'S STRENGTH

Those who destroy the opponent are enraged.
Those who take hold of the opponent can take advantage of their resources.

Thus, during a Challenge,
Reward those who are able to seize ten vehicles or more;
Change the banners and flags of the seized vehicles and incorporate them;
Treat captives well and train them.

This is known as using a triumph over the opponent
To enhance one's own strength.

Among Strategies, therefore,
The best triumph is a swift one.

Therefore, leaders who understand Strategy
Preside over the destiny of the people,
And determine the stability or instability of the organization.

THE
PLAN OF ATTACK

(DEVELOPING AN ERROR-FREE STRATEGY)

SUN TZU BELIEVED THAT A COMPLETE AND LASTING TRIUMPH comes only through a sophisticated strategy, one that acts persuasively on the mind of the opponent. Brilliant leaders are able to bend the will of their opponents without ever engaging in conflict. They Plan their strategy so that their own triumph is inevitable, obvious, and ultimately expected. This winning strategy emerges from a thorough evaluation of one's opponent and a complete understanding of oneself. Sun Tzu pointed out: "Know the other and know yourself: one hundred challenges without danger; know not the other and yet know yourself: one triumph for one defeat; know not the other and know not yourself: every challenge is certain peril."

Sun Tzu described the Attack of an area that is already fortified, or a confrontation with an opponent who is larger or more powerful, as a tactical error that brings certain defeat. He also warned against the mistakes of leaders who formulate Plans that cannot be carried out realistically. Unrealistic tactical Planning will throw a strategy into chaos and give the opponent the advantage. Sun Tzu said: "This is what is meant by a disordered Force leading to another's triumph."

CONFLICT IN THE SELF   Once you have recognized an inner conflict and analyzed the emotional costs in confronting it, it is time to formulate a realistic Plan. The strategy you choose depends upon whether this conflict can be isolated in order to confront it, or whether it is actually the tip of an iceberg that extends deeply into other parts of your life.

If your inner conflict is one that can be isolated, such as a habit you wish to break or a fear that you must overcome, then a direct Attack with unrelenting forward momentum is the sure way of lasting triumph. If, however, your inner conflict is one that is woven into other areas of your personality, such as a destructive attitude or character flaw, a direct confrontation will only exhaust your resources. Therefore, a broader long-term strategy must be developed to turn the entire situation around.

Learn as much as you can about your inner opponent, its patterns of response, and the other parts your life it affects. All of these areas must be identified and acted on simultaneously if victory is to be won. Constant awareness and strategic reprogramming are the keys to transcending deeply rooted inner opponents.

CONFLICT IN THE ENVIRONMENT   A conflict in the environment (such as a stifling career or destructive surroundings) may seem much more formidable than the individual challenging it. What is being challenged, however, is not the environment but your participation in it. Can you adapt to your environment or change your relationship to it so that it fulfills your needs? If not, then use it to propel you onward.

A direct Attack on an ongoing environment brings into action all of the tactical errors that Sun Tzu described. An environment is larger and more powerful than you are. It is a fortified area — fortified because many others have an investment in it, just the way it is, or it could not continue to exist. Thus, a direct Attack on an environment is unlikely to succeed. Strong environments are like strong immune systems, which swiftly eradicate rogue cells.

To overcome an environmental conflict, develop your strategy by carefully analyzing your environment: How does it function? Why does it continue? What happens or does not happen to individuals involved with it? Then study yourself: Why are you involved? Where do you want to be? What steps must you take to get there? The answers to these questions will help you formulate a Plan — one that can show you the way to take your life where you want it to go.

CONFLICT WITH ANOTHER   Interpersonal conflicts are highly emotional and are strongly connected to other parts of your life — to your health, career, and personal growth. Which is stronger and more powerful: your determination to end the conflict or your fear of losing the relationship? In order to triumph over the conflict, you must understand thoroughly your motivations, for they describe your destiny.

If you are unsure of your determination, then your opponent is evidently the stronger one. Thus, it will be necessary to wait until your determination grows and the balance of power is reversed before you can formulate and execute a winning strategy. If, on the other hand, you are certain of your determination, then victory over the conflict is assured — although you should realize that your victory over an nonnegotiable conflict will very likely end the relationship as you know it.

Self-examination is most important here because of the tendency to be attracted to the same personality types and the same problems again and again. Regardless of the reason for this behavior, the best defense is an acute awareness of the pattern. Hidden inside this awareness is the key to developing a triumphant strategy.

CONFLICT AMONG LEADERS   The objective of a skilled, intelligent leader during an interorganizational conflict is to triumph over the rival organization without destroying its resources. To achieve this, a leader must act on the opposing organization in its entirety, using carefully gathered intelligence to anticipate and neutralize destructive resistance.

Of course, a more powerful organization can achieve a sweeping victory through direct Attack, but skillful leaders generally reject this tactic, since it diminishes the resources of the entire system and destroys what may become a "future customer." Brilliant leaders are always aware of the entire system, both inside and outside of their organizations. They know that to harm or destroy what is outside will hurt their own growth, while employing their rivals and incorporating their resources will enhance their strategy.

Once an organization is set in motion to challenge another, skillful leaders do not interfere with the work of specialists who are employed to execute the strategy. To introduce unrealistic tactics, bureaucratic policies, or incompetent team leaders will compromise the strength of the organization. It is through this kind of internal error that powerful organizations are toppled by smaller contenders.

孫子曰：

凡用兵之法，全國爲上，破國次之；全軍爲上，破軍次之；全旅爲上，破旅次之；全卒爲上，破卒次之；全伍爲上，破伍次之。

是故百戰百勝，非善之善者也，不戰而屈人之兵，善之善者也。

故上兵伐謀，其次伐交，其次伐兵，其下攻城。

攻城之法，爲不得已。修櫓轒轀，具器械，三月而後成；距闉，又三月而後已。將不勝其忿，而蟻附之，殺士三分之一，而城不拔者，此攻之災也。

故善用兵者，屈人之兵，而非戰也；拔人之城，而非攻也；毀人之國，而非久也。

必以全爭於天下，故兵不頓，而利可全。

此謀攻之法也。

ENGAGING THE ENTIRE SYSTEM

Sun Tzu said:

Generally, in the execution of an Artful Strategy,
To act on an entire organization is ideal; to break an organization is inferior.
To act on an entire corps is ideal; to break a corps is inferior.
To act on an entire company is ideal; to break a company is inferior.
To act on an entire team is ideal; to break a team is inferior.
To act on an entire unit is ideal; to break a unit is inferior.

Thus, those who win one hundred triumphs in one hundred conflicts
Do not have supreme skill.
Those who have supreme skill,
Use Strategy to bend others without coming to conflict.

The ideal Strategy, therefore, is to thwart a Plan.
The next best is to thwart a Negotiation.
The next best is to thwart a Strategy.
The inferior politic is to Attack a Fortified Area.

Attacking a Fortified Area is an Art of last resort:
It takes three months to complete the preparations
Of armored vehicles, tools, and talent;
It takes three months longer to position a gate in the wall.
Furious leaders will not triumph, but will swarm, ant-like,
So that one third of their Force will be destroyed —
And still the Fortification will not be uprooted.
This is the catastrophe of such an Attack.

Those who are skilled in executing a Strategy,
Bend the strategy of others without conflict;
Uproot the Fortifications of others without Attacking;
Absorb the organizations of others without prolonged operations.

It is essential to engage completely with the Entire System.
Thus the Strategy is never-ending and the gains are complete.

Such is the Art of the Plan of Attack.

The term *Entire System* comes from the ideograms for "below heaven,"
and generally refers to an empire and its civilization.
It is also translated as "world" or "all under heaven."

故用兵之法：

十則圍之，五則攻之，
倍則分之。

敵則能戰之。

少則能守之，
不若則能避之。

故小敵之堅，大敵之擒也。

THE RULE OF NUMBERS

In executing an Artful Strategy:

When ten times greater,
Surround them;
When five times greater,
Attack them;
When two times greater,
Scatter them.

If the opponent is ready to challenge:

When fewer in number,
Be ready to evade them;
When unequal to the match,
Be ready to avoid them.

Even when smaller opponents have a strong position,
The larger opponent will capture them.

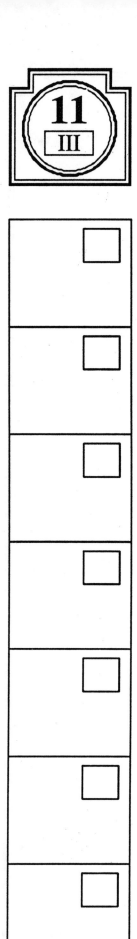

夫將者，國之輔也，輔周則國必強，輔隙則國必弱。

故君之所以患於軍者三：

不知軍之不可以進，而謂之進；不知軍之不可以退，而謂之退，是謂縻軍。

不知三軍之事，而同三軍之政，則軍士惑矣。

不知三軍之權，而同三軍之任，則軍士疑矣。

三軍既惑且疑，則諸侯之難至矣。

是謂亂軍引勝。

THREE ERRORS OF LEADERS

Leaders are those who protect the organization.
If the protection is complete, the organization will be strong.
If the protection is flawed, the organization will be vulnerable.

A Ruler can bring adversity to the Force in three ways:

By not understanding that the Force is unable to advance
And calling for an advance;
Or not understanding that the Force is unable to retreat,
And calling for a retreat.
This is called hobbling the Force.

By not understanding the Work of the Entire Force
And aligning the Entire Force along political lines.
As a result, individuals in the Force become doubtful.

By not understanding the natural authority of the Entire Force
And aligning the Entire Force with appointed officials.
As a result, individuals in the Force become skeptical.

When the Entire Force is doubtful, and moreover, skeptical,
Other leaders can cause serious problems.

This is what is meant by a disordered Force leading to another's triumph.

The word *Ruler* comes from the Chinese word *chun*,
which can be translated as "monarch" or "king."
It refers to the highest authority, such as a government and its laws and charters.

The term *Entire Force* comes from the ideograms for "three forces,"
and refers to the military troop formations of advance, backup, and main divisions.

故知勝有五：

知可以與戰，不可以與戰者勝；

識眾寡之用者勝；

上下同欲者勝；

以虞待不虞者勝；

將能而君不御者勝。

此五者知勝之道也。

故曰：知彼知己，百戰不殆；不知彼而知己，一勝一負；不知彼不知己，每戰必殆。

THE ESSENTIALS OF TRIUMPH

There are Five ways triumph can be known:

Those who know when to challenge and when not to challenge will triumph.
Those who recognize how to use the numerous and the few will triumph.
Those who agree on superior and inferior objectives will triumph.
Those who prepare to lie in wait for the unprepared will triumph.
Those who lead without interference from a Ruler will triumph.

Those who know these Five, as well as the Tao, will triumph.

Thus, it is said:
"Know the other and know yourself:
One hundred challenges without danger;
Know not the other and yet know yourself:
One triumph for one defeat;
Know not the other and know not yourself:
Every challenge is certain peril."

C H A P T E R   F O U R

POSITIONING

(POSITIONING YOURSELF FOR TRIUMPH)

"THOSE WHO ARE SKILLED IN CONFLICT," SAID SUN TZU, "establish a Situation that cannot be defeated and miss no opportunity to defeat their opponent." This simple formula for winning through Positioning is one of the foundations of *The Art of Strategy*. With skillful Positioning, defeat or triumph is apparent to everyone involved, well in advance of any confrontation. For a skilled strategist, triumph is effortless and confrontation is finally an unnecessary exercise to prove the point. Sun Tzu believed that to challenge another without the complete certainty of emerging victorious is the mark of an inferior strategist.

Sun Tzu described a strategy of Positioning that must be carefully executed in order to assure victory. Skillful strategists put themselves beyond attack by becoming invisible, seamless, without error. At the same time, they gather intelligence and analyze it in light of their objectives. They move in the same direction as the larger trends in their world, so that they can harness the timeliness of that momentum. Then they wait for their opponent to move, for well-Positioned strategists are led to triumph through the actions of their opponents.

CONFLICT IN THE SELF   Many inner conflicts, such as character flaws that block motivation or achievement, are too large to be attacked directly. For some reason, this inner opponent has been given a place in your life, and that place must be taken away. Situate your inner opponent out of your life by adjusting your own Position in the world. Use the world around you to make your triumph as effortless as possible by observing and aligning yourself with social trends or modes of conduct that support your goals. Focus on these and allow their influence to strengthen your determination.

Secure your defenses against dangerous setbacks by removing any elements from your surroundings that may contribute to the problem. Look for support in your environment and in your society, and use it to reinforce your self-discipline. If your goal is a healthy one but your environment is unsupportive, you may have an environmental conflict to deal with, as well.

If you are unsure of your determination and the inevitability of your triumph, hold back and wait until your Position is improved. Just as the steel of a sword is hardened with intermittent heat, a false start will make your inner opponent stronger. Only when your plan is in Position and you are certain of your triumph over your inner opponent should you execute your strategy.

CONFLICT IN THE ENVIRONMENT   In developing a strategy to overcome an environmental conflict, Positioning is your most effective tactic. Environments may be large and strong, but they are stationary and their Position is always apparent. Your advantage over such a powerful opponent is your flexibility and your ability to conceal your plan.

Never move against an environment until you are able to rise above it successfully. To assure success, you must secure yourself against attack by being without error, by remaining invisible. At the same time, you must prepare to move quickly when the opportunity presents itself. Sun Tzu said: "Those who are skilled in defense are as invisible as the lowest on earth. Those who are skilled in attack can move with the highest in heaven. Therefore, they are protected while gaining a complete triumph."

Although tremendous planning and work must go into strategic Positioning, a lasting triumph over your environmental conflict will seem perfectly natural when it finally occurs. To help make your transition smooth and faultless, study carefully your new destination and align yourself to its rhythms, patterns, and principles well in advance of any action.

CONFLICT WITH ANOTHER   Overcoming interpersonal conflicts is a transactional martial art with a three-step strategy: Study your opponent and the patterns of the conflict; Position yourself so that you are protected and your opponent is exposed; then wait for your opponent to act. Sun Tzu said: "Those who are skilled in conflict can secure themselves against defeat, but it is their opponent who provides the opportunity for triumph."

The second step of this strategy, Positioning, is fundamental to victory. To Position yourself, make certain that you act with integrity, that your actions are above reproach, that you are blameless. In this way, you cannot be attacked during the execution of your plan. While keeping your Position invisible and error-free, focus your energy and awareness on your opponent's actions to expose any weakness or compromised integrity.

Only detached, methodical, determined planning will result in a lasting triumph. Emotional heat and hasty reactions will undermine your strategy and lead to increased conflict. In overcoming conflicts you will write the scenario to reflect your objectives; but it is your opponent who must act it out. When the strategy is executed properly, the triumph will be apparent to everyone.

CONFLICT AMONG LEADERS   Strategic Positioning will not only assure triumph in interorganizational conflicts, but it can bring this victory about without wasteful struggles or expensive confrontations. Only the most evolved leader will achieve this ideal triumph, because the art of Positioning is a silent strategy. There are no heroes and no rewards, and there can be no mistakes.

A strategically Positioned organization is not open to attack, because it is not engaged in unprincipled activities and its profile is kept purposefully low. The organization's defense is secured and protected through its integrity. It is this low Position that highlights the actions of the rival organization, bringing into the spotlight its flaws and weaknesses.

Sun Tzu pointed out: "Those who are skilled in the use of Strategy cultivate the Tao to secure their Art. Hence, triumph or defeat can come through political actions." Brilliant leaders align themselves and their organizations with the larger trends and evolving sentiments of society. In this way, they reinforce the strength and Position of their organization and gain a broad negotiating advantage.

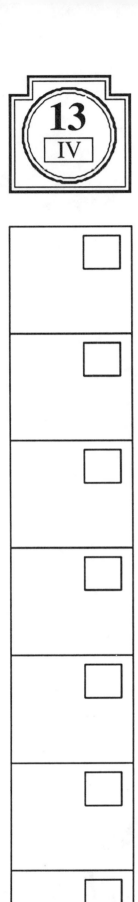

孫子曰：

昔之善戰者，先爲不可勝，以待敵之可勝。

不可勝在己，可勝在敵。

故善戰者，能爲不可勝，不能使敵必可勝。

故曰：勝可知而不可爲。

不可勝者，守也；可勝者，攻也。

守則不足，攻則有餘。

善守者藏於九地之下；善攻者動於九天之上，

故能自保而全勝也。

THE POWER DEFENSE

Sun Tzu said:

In Ancient Times,
Those who were skilled in conflict put themselves beyond defeat
And awaited their opponent's reach for triumph.

To secure against defeat depends on oneself;
The opportunity for triumph depends on one's opponent.

Therefore, those who are skilled in conflict
Can secure themselves against defeat,
But it is their opponent who provides the opportunity for triumph.

Hence it is said:
"One may know how to triumph
And yet may not be able to manage it."

Those who cannot triumph should defend;
Those who can triumph may attack.
Defend when there are inadequacies;
Attack when there is surplus.

Those who are skilled in defense
Are as invisible as the lowest on earth.
Those who are skilled in attack
Can move with the highest in heaven.
Therefore, they are protected while gaining a complete triumph.

The terms *lowest on earth* and *highest in heaven* come from the ideograms for
"ninth layer of earth" and "ninth layer of heaven."
These terms refer to the unique forces of the most minute life forms
and to the overwhelming power of the physical laws.

見勝不過眾人之所知，非善之善者也。

戰勝而天下曰善，非善之善者也。

故舉秋毫不爲多力。見日月不爲明目。聞雷霆不爲聰耳。

古之所謂善戰者，勝易勝者也。

THE TRIUMPH OF NO EFFORT

Those who are aware of triumph
When it is obvious also to the multitudes,
Do not have excellent skills.

Those who triumph during conflict
While the world says, "Well done!"
Do not have excellent skills.

To lift an autumn leaf is not an act of great strength.
To see the sun and moon is not an act of sharp sight.
To hear a sudden thunderclap is not an act of acute listening.

Those whom the Ancient Ones called "Skilled in Conflict,"
Are those who triumph because triumph is easy.

故善戰者之勝也，無智名，無勇功。

故其戰勝不忒。

不忒者，其所措必勝，勝已敗者也。

故善戰者，立於不敗之地，而不失敵之敗也。

THE POSITION OF NO ERROR

Those who triumph because they are skilled in conflict
Are not honored for cleverness
Or credited for heroism.

They triumph during conflict because they have made no errors.

Those who have made no errors
Have arranged for certain triumph:
A triumph over those who are already defeated.

Therefore, those who are skilled in conflict
Establish a Situation that cannot be defeated,
And miss no opportunity to defeat their opponent.

是故勝兵先勝而後求戰，敗兵先戰而後求勝。

善用兵者，修道而保法，故能爲勝敗之政。

兵法：一曰度，二曰量，三曰數，四曰稱，五曰勝。

地生度，度生量，量生數，數生稱，稱生勝。

故勝兵若以鎰稱銖，敗兵若以銖稱鎰。

勝者之戰人也，若決積水於千仞之谿者，

形也。

THE FIVE STRATEGIC ARTS

Winning Strategists are certain of triumph
Before seeking a challenge.
Losing Strategists are certain to challenge
Before seeking a triumph.

Those who are skilled in the use of Strategy,
Cultivate the Tao to secure their Art.
Hence, triumph or defeat can come through political actions.

The Strategic Arts are
First, measurements;
Second, estimates;
Third, analysis;
Fourth, balancing;
Fifth, triumph.

The Situation gives rise to measurements.
Measurements give rise to estimates.
Estimates give rise to analysis.
Analysis gives rise to balancing.
Balance gives rise to triumph.

Therefore, a winning Strategy is like a pound balanced against an ounce,
While a losing Strategy is like an ounce balanced against a pound.
Those who triumph when challenging others
Are like pent-up waters that seem to burst through a thousand-foot gorge.

Such is Positioning.

The word *ounce* can be literally translated as "one twentieth of a tael."
The word *pound* refers to a whole tael.
In China, a tael is any of various units of value based on weight.

CHAPTER FIVE

DIRECTING

(POSITIONING YOUR OPPONENT FOR DEFEAT)

*S*UN TZU BELIEVED THAT THE IDEAL STRATEGY DURING CON-flict is to move opponents here and there, until they are perfectly positioned to their own disadvantage. This strategy, which he called Directing, is the art of compelling the opponent to react to whatever information is presented. It is a skill that is used by leaders who are gifted with creative, insightful minds. While Directing can be used to carefully position the opponent, leaders must also be masters of timing, for it is strategic timing that makes Directing effective.

Sun Tzu referred to the principal forces in Directing as the surprising and the straightforward. He said: "Generally, in a conflict, the Straightforward will lead to engagement and the Surprising will lead to triumph." Sun Tzu believed that these tactics could be used, in endless variations, to orchestrate the ideal victory — one that is uneventful and nondestructive. To use surprise, skillful leaders create the appearance of confusion, fear, or vulnerability, causing the opponent to perceive a false weakness. The opponent is helplessly drawn toward this illusion of advantage. As Sun Tzu pointed out: "Through the promise of gain, an opponent is moved about while the Team lies in wait."

CONFLICT IN THE SELF   The first step in challenging an internal conflict is to isolate the problem from other parts of your life. Cut the ties that bind it to your personal growth or motivation. Reposition your inner conflict outside your agenda by making plans for your life that do not include it. Do not attack your inner opponent directly. Isolate it instead by visualizing it apart from yourself.

Now is a good time to enlist the help of others. When you convince those around you that the conflict will be overcome, it strengthens that idea, giving it weight and reinforcement. Sun Tzu said that "those skilled in conflict who Direct through others seem to travel like a rounded boulder down a thousand-meter mountain."

Timing is another factor to keep in mind while executing your strategy. Because you are positioning yourself apart from your conflict, opportunities will present themselves to draw you even farther away. Sometimes these opportunities will take you in unexpected directions — perhaps even to areas of new interest that could hold the solution to your problem. Begin to act spontaneously. In this way you are enlisting the tactical advantage of surprise to overcome your inner opponent.

CONFLICT IN THE ENVIRONMENT   An open confrontation will trigger overpowering resistance from your environment. Thus, the key to triumph in an environmental conflict is the ability to use surprise tactics. Environments, both large and small, continually work to protect themselves from individuals who will not conform. Therefore, it is only when the environment feels no threat from you that it has been properly Directed and positioned for your strategy.

As you develop a strategy that will help you transcend this conflict, you will grow stronger, more determined, and more apart from your environment. With your growing detachment you will acquire a new attitude about your environment and its place in your life. Look at it in terms of the past, not the future. In this way you turn your environmental conflict into a springboard instead of a barrier.

Remember, when you change your environment or your relationship to it, your place in the world and your ultimate destiny will also change. The opportunity for a transition of this magnitude is difficult to arrange, so when the time comes to act, you must do so without hesitation. Be very clear beforehand about the strength of your determination and understand, as thoroughly as you can, your objective or projected destination.

CONFLICT WITH ANOTHER   The strategy for overcoming interpersonal conflicts is largely one of positioning yourself for victory and positioning your conflict for defeat. The position of victory is one of determination and detachment; the position of defeat is unpreparedness. Remember, this is not a negotiation to adjust an aspect of incompatibility in your relationship, it is a strategy designed to completely neutralize an unresolvable life-damaging conflict.

Begin to Direct your opponent's position well in advance of any confrontation. If you are involved in a relationship where the pattern of conflict repeats, begin your Directing before the next peak. When the same conflict occurs regularly, it means that your communications are ineffective and the relationship must be completely altered.

Conceal your strategy from your opponent as you build your strength and determination. The influence of your nonconfrontive posture will Direct your opponent into a deluded position — the position of defeat. If possible, you may want to employ outside help in executing your strategy. Supportive allies can corroborate the impression you are transmitting to your opponent. They can also reinforce your determination and witness your triumph.

CONFLICT AMONG LEADERS   During a time of interorganizational conflict, skillful leaders are able to manipulate the opposing organization by continually forcing it to readjust its position. Brilliant leaders project strategic misinformation about their own position, and feign tactical vulnerabilities that lure the opponent into a desired area. Sun Tzu pointed out: "Skillfulness in moving the opponent about comes through positioning that the opponent is compelled to follow and gifts the opponent is compelled to take."

Once the rival organization is properly positioned and its focus has been Directed to fit the strategy, a leader must seize the moment and act quickly. During conflict, everything is in motion, so decisive timing is vital to an effective strategy. "Direction," said Sun Tzu, "is like a tautly drawn crossbow; timing is like the release of the arrow."

Superior leaders call on a powerful resource in tactical Directing by using their own organization to create the effect they wish to project, whether it is the appearance of vulnerability and confusion or of strength and infallibility. An opponent can be greatly influenced by a well-orchestrated strategy of illusion. Because skillful leaders generally do not inform individuals in their organization of this strategy, these individuals are never compromised and are always beyond blame or reproach.

孫子曰：

凡治衆如治寡。

分數是也。

鬪衆如鬪寡。

形名是也。

三軍之衆，可使必受敵而無敗者。

奇正是也。

兵之所加，如以碬投卵者。

虛實是也。

THE POSITIONED STRATEGY

Sun Tzu said:

Generally, the control of the numerous
Is like the control of the few.

It is a matter of planning the divisions.

A contest with the numerous
Is like a contest with the few.

It is a matter of masterful Positioning.

The Entire Force must be able to act on the opponent
Without sustaining losses.

It is a matter of the Surprising and the Straightforward.

The impact that comes from a Strategy
Is like an egg thrown against a millstone.

It is a matter of Illusion and Reality.

The terms *Surprising* and *Straightforward* come from the ideograms *ch'i* and *cheng*.
As a military concept, *ch'i* refers to a surprise attack or ambush, and *cheng* to a direct offensive.
The combination of these maneuvers is an important principle in Chinese military strategy.

凡戰者，以正合，以奇勝。

故善出奇者，無窮如天地，不竭若江河。終而復始，日月是也；死而復生，四時是也。

聲不過五；五聲之變，不可勝聽也。色不過五；五色之變，不可勝觀也。味不過五；五味之變，不可勝嘗也。

戰勢不過奇正；奇正之變，不可勝窮也。

奇正相生，如循環之無端，孰能窮之？

THE POWER OF SURPRISE

Generally, in a conflict,
The Straightforward will lead to engagement and
The Surprising will lead to triumph.

Thus, those who are skilled in producing surprises
Are as infinitely varied as heaven and earth,
And as inexhaustible as the great rivers.
Like the sun and moon,
They come to an end and cycle to the beginning.
Like the four seasons,
They expire and cycle through to rebirth.

There are no more than five tones,
Yet five tones excel in Variations — more than can ever be heard.
There are no more than five colors,
Yet five colors excel in Variations— more than can ever be seen.
There are no more than five flavors,
Yet five flavors excel in Variations — more than can ever be tasted.

In Directing a conflict,
There are no more than the Surprising and the Straightforward,
Yet the Surprising and the Straightforward excel in Variations —
More than can ever be exhausted.

The Surprising and the Straightforward give rise to each other
As they rotate and cycle without end.
Who can exhaust them?

The term *great rivers* comes from the two characters for the Yangtze and the Yellow rivers.
These rivers are China's largest and most important waterways.

激水之疾，至於漂石者，勢也。鷙鳥之疾，至於毀折者，節也。

是故善戰者，其勢險，其節短。

勢如彍弩，節如發機。

紛紛紜紜，鬬亂而不可亂也；渾渾沌沌，形圓而不可敗也。

亂生於治，怯生於勇，弱生於強。

治亂，數也；勇怯，勢也；強弱，形也。

故善動敵者，形之，敵必從之；予之，敵必取之。

以利動之，以卒待之。

MOVING THE OPPONENT ABOUT

Those who have Direction can arouse like charging waters,
Uprooting boulders along the way.
Those who have Timing can charge like a bird of prey,
Piercing its target along the way.

Hence, those who are skilled in conflict
Are formidable in their Directing and quick in their Timing.

Directing is like a tautly drawn crossbow;
Timing is like the release of the arrow.

The numbers and confusions and comings and goings
Make the contest seem disordered —
And yet there is no disorder.
The blending and merging and chaos and tumult
Make the Position seem encircled —
And yet there is no losing.

Apparent disorder is a product of control.
Apparent fear is a product of courage.
Apparent vulnerability is a product of possession.

Control or disorder is a matter of Analysis.
Courage or fear is a matter of Direction.
Possession or vulnerability is a matter of Positioning.

Skillfulness in moving an opponent about comes through
Positioning the opponent is compelled to follow
And gifts the opponent is compelled to take.

Through the promise of gain,
An opponent is moved about
While the Team lies in wait.

故善戰者，求之於勢，不責於人，故能擇人而任勢。

任勢者，其戰人也，如轉木石；木石之性，安則靜，危則動，方則止，圓則行。

故善戰人之勢，如轉圓石於千仞之山者，勢也。

USING OTHERS TO CREATE MOMENTUM

Those who are skilled in conflict seek to Direct without blaming others.
Hence, they can select others and employ them in Directing.

Those who employ others in Directing a conflict
Seem to travel like timber and boulders.
It is the nature of timber and boulders
To be still when stable,
To move when unstable;
To stop when squared,
To move when rounded.

Those skilled in conflict
Who Direct through others,
Seem to travel like a rounded boulder
Down a thousand-meter mountain.

Such is Directing.

The term *meter* comes from the Chinese word *jen*, which is actually a measure of length
equaling approximately eight feet.

CHAPTER SIX

ILLUSION
AND REALITY

(USING CAMOUFLAGE)

$\mathcal{T}$HE IDEA OF CREATING ILLUSIONS TO OBSCURE REALITY IS A specific tactical maneuver designed to keep the opponent at a constant disadvantage. Sun Tzu emphasized the use of Illusion throughout *The Art of Strategy*, and believed that leaders who understood and employed this technique were invincible. About such leaders he exclaimed: "Subtle! Intangible! Seemingly without Shape. Mysterious! Miraculous! Seemingly without Sound. They master the destiny of their opponents."

Brilliant leaders use creative Illusion in all of their strategies — Illusions that cause the opponent to lose perspective and make mistakes. They never allow an opponent to ascertain their position, and in this way they compel their opponent to prepare a defense in every area. In effect, they are dividing their opponent's forces. Skillful leaders always arrive early for meetings and engagements so that they are prepared before others arrive. Moreover, they build spontaneity into their strategy so that they continually force their opponents to readjust. When the burden of reaction is on the opponent, their resources are taxed and their inadequacies are subtly revealed.

CONFLICT IN THE SELF   Once a challenge is begun, an inner opponent must never be given time to rest and recuperate. Your inner conflict must never be far from your awareness as you continually gauge its hold on your life and keep it in constant retreat. Continual forward momentum and the "wearing down" of your problem is the key to eradicating it permanently.

Anticipate your inner opponent. Know where or when it is likely to surface and be there first with distractions and diversions. Your inner conflict developed because you have, at one time, given it some control in your life. Now you must take that away. Sun Tzu said: "Take the initiative over others so that others do not take the initiative."

Your inner opponent cannot survive long without your support. When you continually refuse to yield to it, it will expire. If it is given a respite, however, its strength will return and your challenge must begin once again. Therefore, your determination is of critical importance, for only a strategy that is constant and vigilant will triumph completely.

CONFLICT IN THE ENVIRONMENT   An environment is a large and powerful entity with nearly inexhaustible resources. The Reality of its position, however, happens to be your chief advantage in challenging it. Because your environment is fixed in time and space, you can move freely through it, gathering intelligence to help you determine its strength, its limitations, and its control in your life.

Do not allow your environment to focus on you. Keep your profile low by creating the Illusion of conformity. This will allow you to execute your strategy in your own time and on your own terms. If you, as an individual, are to overcome your conflict by controlling your environment, you must develop a strategy to divide its strength into smaller, more manageable units. Sun Tzu believed that although the large generally triumph over the small, these odds can be reversed through Illusion. He suggested that obscuring the location where our strategy is unfolding would force our opponent's defenses to be everywhere at once, thinly divided. "When the opponent is Positioned, we must appear without Position," he said. "As a result, we are numerous and the opponent is few."

When your environment is clearly your opponent, you may be in an unresolvable crisis. Attempting to reposition yourself in an unsuitable environment can be a lifetime occupation, and adapting to an unsuitable environment can be a life-defeating compromise. Therefore, it is important to carefully plan a viable destination before engaging in an environmental challenge.

CONFLICT WITH ANOTHER   During interpersonal challenges, it is vital to learn as much as you possibly can about your opponent. By creating Illusions to which your opponent must react, you can discover weaknesses, strengths, blind spots, and areas of confidence. You can then use this information in developing your strategy.

Once your interpersonal challenge has begun you must keep your opponent unsure and in constant readjustment. Most important, you must continually obscure your plan and your attitudes. In this way, you protect yourself from attack while the confusion you create depletes your opponent's resources: An opponent who is not certain of your position cannot attack, and instead must prepare defenses in every area.

Remember, you are not fighting to see who has the best position. In interpersonal challenges you are struggling to overcome an unresolvable conflict. Once a challenge is begun it must be continued, without rest, until the the conflict is eradicated or the relationship completely altered.

CONFLICT AMONG LEADERS   Sun Tzu believed that leaders who are skilled in the use of Illusion during interorganizational conflicts are certain to triumph. Skillful leaders systematically obscure their position and their plan in order to protect themselves from the strategies of their adversaries. Sun Tzu said: "Without Position, even the deepest intelligence is unable to spy; and those who are clever are unable to Plan."

Illusion is a highly effective intelligence-gathering tool for organizations. Experimental posturing can provoke quick reactions from others — reactions that, when carefully analyzed, will reveal the strengths and weaknesses, the folly or creativity of others. Once these are known, a skillful leader may advance confidently. "Those whose advances are unstoppable," said Sun Tzu, "forge ahead with Illusion."

Skillful leaders enhance the strength of their own organizations by compelling their opponents to divide their resources into smaller, widely scattered units. The true size and strength of an organization is thus a function of its ability to manipulate its rivals' resources of money, creativity, or manpower. By obscuring the area of their potential confrontation, skilled leaders force their adversaries to prepare in many places at once. Sun Tzu said: "When opponents must prepare in many places, there will be few at the location where we initiate a challenge."

孫子曰：

凡先處戰地而待敵者佚，後處戰地而趨戰者勞。

故善戰者，致人，而不致於人。

能使敵人自至者，利之也；能使敵人不得至者，害之也。

故敵佚能勞之，飽能饑之，安能動之。

出其所不趨，趨其所不意。行千里而不勞者，行於無人之地也。

CREATING IMBALANCE

Sun Tzu said:

Generally, those who occupy the place of conflict early,
Can face their opponent in comfort.
Those who occupy the place of conflict late,
Must hasten into conflict troubled.

Thus, those who are skilled in conflict,
Take the initiative over others
So that others do not take the initiative.

Opponents can be self-directed to approach
Through the promise of advantage.
Opponents can be self-directed to hesitate
Through the promise of disadvantage.

Therefore, when opponents are comfortable, they should be troubled;
When satisfied, they should be starved;
When calm, they should be moved.

Move first to locations where they must hasten.
Hasten to locations they do not expect.
Those who can travel a thousand miles without trouble,
Travel where others are not situated.

攻而必取者，攻其所不守也。守而必固者，守其所不攻也。

故善攻者，敵不知其所守；善守者，敵不知其所攻。

微乎微乎，至於無形；神乎神乎，至於無聲，故能為敵之司命。

進而不可禦者，衝其虛也；退而不可追者，速而不可及也。

故我欲戰，敵雖高壘深溝，不得不與我戰者，攻其所必救也。

我不欲戰，畫地而守之，敵不得與我戰者，乖其所之也。

故形人而我無形，則我專而敵分。

我專為一，敵分為十，是以十攻其一也，則我眾而敵寡。

能以眾擊寡者，則我之所與戰者約矣。

DISTORTING THE OPPONENT'S POSITION

Those who are certain to capture what is attacked,
Attack locations that are not defended.
Those who are certain to secure what is defended,
Defend locations that cannot be attacked.

Thus, an opponent does not know what location to defend
Against those skilled in attack.
Nor does an opponent know what location to attack
Against those skilled in defense.

Subtle! Intangible! Seemingly without Shape.
Mysterious! Miraculous! Seemingly without Sound.
They master the destiny of their opponents.

Those whose advances are unstoppable, forge ahead with Illusion.
Those whose retreats cannot be pursued, are too fast to be reached.

Therefore, if we want to challenge an opponent,
Despite towering walls and deep waterways,
Challenge so the opponent cannot help but engage:
Attack a location the opponent is compelled to rescue.

If we do not want a challenge,
When our defense is but a boundary line,
Challenge so that the opponent is unable to engage:
Distort the opponent's sense of location.

Thus, when the opponent is Positioned, we must appear without Position.
As a result, we may focus while the opponent must divide.

Focused we may act as One, while the opponent must divide by ten.
Therefore, we are One-united and the opponent is one tenth.
As a result, we are numerous and the opponent is few.

Because those who are numerous can always take those who are few,
We must be appropriately Positioned to engage in the challenge.

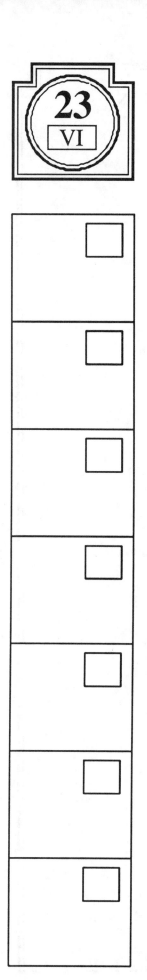

吾所與戰之地不可知，不可知，則敵所備者多，敵所備者多，則吾所與戰者寡矣。

故備前則後寡，備後則前寡，備左則右寡，備右則左寡，無所不備，則無所不寡。

寡者，備人者也；眾者，使人備己者也。

故知戰之地，知戰之日，則可千里而會戰。不知戰地，不知戰日，則左不能救右，右不能救左，前不能救後，後不能救前，而況遠者數十里，近者數里乎！

以吾度之，越人之兵雖多，亦奚益於勝敗哉？故曰：勝可爲也。

敵雖眾，可使無鬥。故策之而知得失之計，作之而知動靜之理，形之而知死生之地，角之而知有餘不足之處。

ADJUSTING THE OPPONENT'S NUMBERS

The location we take to initiate a challenge must not be made known.
When opponents do not know our location,
They must prepare in many places.
When opponents must prepare in many places,
There will be few at the location where we initiate a challenge.

Hence, when the front is prepared, there are fewer in back.
When the back is prepared, there are fewer in front.
When the left is prepared, there are fewer on the right.
When the right is prepared, there are fewer on the left.
When every location is prepared, every location will have fewer in place.

Those who are fewer are those who prepare against others.
Those who are numerous are those who make others prepare against them.

Therefore, when the time and place of a challenge is known,
One can meet the challenge from a thousand miles away.
But when the time and place of a challenge is not known,
The left cannot rescue the right,
The right cannot rescue the left,
The front cannot rescue the back,
The back cannot rescue the front.
This is more so for those at a distance of several hundred miles,
And even so for those who are as near as a few miles!

If, through measuring the Strategy of others,
We find their numbers to exceed our own,
Does this advantage indicate triumph or defeat?
It is said: "Triumph can be Managed."

Even when opponents are numerous they can be subdued.
Through maneuvering, learn their calculations for gains and losses.
Through action, learn their policies for movement or silence.
Through Positioning, learn their areas of desperation and security.
Through contact, learn where they possess surplus or inadequacies.

The term *exceed* comes from the Chinese word *yueh*,
which can also be translated as "to go beyond" or "even more."
Yueh is also the name of an ancient state in China, active about 500 B.C.

故形兵之極至於無形，無形則深間不能窺，智者不能謀。

因形而措勝於眾，眾不能知。人皆知我所以勝之形，而莫知我所以制勝之形。

故其戰勝不復，而應形於無窮。

夫兵形象水，水之行，避高而趨下；兵之形，避實而擊虛。水因地而制流；兵因敵而制勝。

故兵無常勢，水無常形，能因敵變化而取勝者，謂之神。

故五行無常勝，四時無常位，日有短長，月有死生。

REACTING WITH SYSTEMATIC POSITIONING

The ultimate Positioned Strategy
Is to be without an apparent Position.
Without Position even the deepest Intelligence is unable to spy;
And those who are clever are unable to Plan.

Intricate Positioning will appear as a triumph to the multitudes,
But the multitudes cannot comprehend it.
Others can comprehend that we have won through Positioning,
But they cannot comprehend that we have won
Through Systematic Positioning.

Thus, once a challenge is won, the System should not be repeated.
Positioning should be a reaction to infinite Variations.

The Strategy of Positioning is the image of water.
Moving water evades heights and hastens through the lowlands;
A Strategy of Positioning evades Reality and confronts through Illusion.
Water follows the territory and Systematically flows;
The Strategy follows the opponent and Systematically triumphs.

Just as water has no absolute Position,
The Strategy has no absolute Direction.
Those who can follow their opponent's transformations to take triumph,
May be called genius.

Thus, among the five elements, none is absolutely dominant.
Among the four seasons, none is absolutely Positioned.
The days may appear long or short;
The moon may wax or wane.

The five elements are metal, wood, water, fire, and earth.
All the elements exist interdependently, hence "none is absolutely dominant."

The word *Intelligence* is from the Chinese word *chien*, which means
a space between two things, a leak or crevice, or a change or substitute.
It can also be translated as "spying" or "espionage."
Since *chien* refers to the information that results from a leak or crevice,
it is translated in *The Art of Strategy* as "Intelligence."
Intelligence-gathering is discussed at length in Chapter Thirteen, "The Use of Intelligence."

CHAPTER SEVEN

ENGAGING THE FORCE

(MANEUVERING FOR ADVANTAGE)

SUN TZU DESCRIBED ENGAGING THE FORCE AS MANEUVERING designed to capture the advantage during a challenge. He suggested that the most successful maneuvering would come through the mastery of direct and indirect tactics — especially the ability to achieve a direct effect through indirect means. He believed that even small adversities for one's opponent can be great opportunities for indirect maneuvering. Those who are disorganized, logistically disadvantaged, worried, or anxious are holding out useful advantages for their opponents. Sun Tzu maintained that a brilliant leader will know how to turn these indirect advantages to victory. "Those who triumph," he said, "know beforehand how to calculate the Direct and Indirect."

Sun Tzu also described a number of pitfalls to avoid while Engaging the Force. Skillful leaders never challenge when their opponents' spirits are high or when their defenses are orderly and impressive. Instead, they lie in wait for the inevitable decline. Furthermore, they are never tempted by their opponents' gifts, nor do they pursue when their opponents feign fear or flight. Again, they wait. Superior leaders never encourage competition within their organizations, for they know this will, in fact, diminish their own resources. Finally, once they do gain the advantage, the most enlightened leaders are careful to give their opponents an exit. Sun Tzu said: "When the opposition withdraws, never interfere; when surrounding the opposition, leave an opening; when the opponent is desperate, never press. Such is the execution of an Artful Strategy."

CONFLICT IN THE SELF   When confronting an inner opponent, you must continually maneuver yourself into the advantageous position. Indirect tactics are vital here. Very often an inner opponent will gain strength from a direct confrontation simply because you have Engaged it and given it recognition. Indirect strategies will allow you to usurp its strength without reinforcing it.

Study your inner opponent to learn its cycles of high and low energy: When it is at low ebb you can move freely and unfold your strategy; when your opponent grows strong, however, you must act indirectly. Employ distractions that lead you away from your conflict. Merely withdrawing your attention from your conflict and focusing it elsewhere can be a lethal indirect weapon during inner confrontations.

Find a focus for your goals — an image of yourself, for instance, peacefully functioning without your conflict. Then develop a simple signal that will remind you of this ideal. In this way, you are protected and your strategy is strengthened through your psychological coordination.

CONFLICT IN THE ENVIRONMENT   Maneuvering for advantage in environmental challenges is primarily a strategy of intelligence-gathering. It should be obvious that your tactics must be indirect, since effective fact-finding will be difficult once your environment is on alert against you. Furthermore, indirect tactics will protect you from undue resistance while your strategy is unfolding.

Research your environment with great care so that you thoroughly understand the system and how it operates. If you can, seek information, however expensive, from those who know. Sun Tzu said, "Those who do not know the positions of the mountains, forests, passes, and marshes are not able to move the Force. Those who do not employ local guides are not able to affect the Situation to advantage."

You must learn in which areas the environment is troubled or vulnerable and in which it is formidable. Moreover, you must discover the times when your environment has the strongest hold on you and when that hold weakens. Use this information to maneuver yourself into an advantageous and disentangled position. From here you can unfold a strategy to provoke reform in your relationship to your environment; or you can allow yourself to step beyond your environment onto another path.

CONFLICT WITH ANOTHER   In interpersonal conflicts there are three factors under your opponent's control that, when carefully monitored, will help you maneuver into a position of advantage. The first is your opponent's spirit, or inner determination. Sun Tzu said: "In the morning the Spirit is sharp; in the daytime the Spirit is idle; at dusk the Sprit draws inward. Hence, those who are skilled in the use of Strategy evade when the Spirit is sharp and confront when the Spirit is idle or withdrawn."

The second factor is composure. To triumph over an interpersonal conflict, you must constantly observe your opponent's composure. Sun Tzu noted that composure is shaken during moments of chaos and confusion, and that such times are ideal for confrontation. He said: "The controlled lie in wait for the disorganized; the calm lie in wait for the disorderly."

Finally, the strength of your opponent will have great bearing on the effectiveness of your strategy. That strength will be most compromised during times when your opponent is at a distance from the center of action, or is anxious to fulfill a need, or when normal routines are upset. When your opponent is compromised in either spirit, composure, or strength, you may Engage your Force and advance successfully.

CONFLICT AMONG LEADERS   Brilliant leaders Engaged in inter-organizational conflicts continually maneuver their Force into the position of advantage. This is an indirect strategy that uses the mistakes, anxieties, or flagging enthusiasm of rivals as opportunities for advancement. Maneuvering for advantage is a strategy that leads to a nondestructive and lasting triumph.

Sun Tzu warned leaders that introducing competitiveness within the organization to spur it on to greater achievement is a dangerous maneuver. When the organization is divided into teams and team leaders, and these groups are compelled to compete with one another, the cooperation and coordination within the organization is hobbled and its survival system is compromised. He said of this: "A Force without significant transportation must lose; one without provisions must lose; one without supply caravans must lose."

Sun Tzu further stated that when the decisive advantage is gained over a rival organization, enlightened leaders do not press on. They hold their position and give their rivals the opportunity to surrender, flee, or merge. They do not Engage with rivals who are desperate, for they will not allow their Force to be damaged by those who have nothing more to lose.

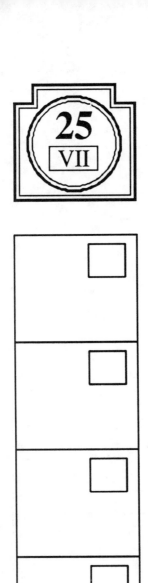

孫子曰：

凡用兵之法，將受命於君。

合軍聚衆，交和而舍。

莫難於軍爭。

軍爭之難者，以迂爲直，以患爲利。

故迂其途，而誘之以利，後人發，先人至。

此知迂直之計者也。

DIRECT AND INDIRECT TACTICS

Sun Tzu said:

Generally, in executing an Artful Strategy,
The Leader is directed by a Ruler.
The Force is gathered, their numbers assembled;
They are united, oriented, and sheltered.

Nothing is as difficult as Engaging the Force.

The difficulties in Engaging the Force
Are those of making the Indirect act Directly
And adversity act as an advantage.

Hence, take the Indirect route;
Lure others by holding out advantages.
Start out after them and arrive before them.

Those who can calculate so
Have mastered the Direct and the Indirect.

故軍爭爲利，軍爭爲危。

舉軍而爭利，則不及；委軍而爭利，則輜重捐。

是故卷甲而趨，日夜不處，倍道兼行，百里而爭利，則擒三將軍。

勁者先，疲者後，其法十一而至。

五十里而爭利，則蹶上將軍，其法半至。

三十里而爭利，則三分之二至。

是故軍無輜重則亡，無糧食則亡，無委積則亡。

AVOIDING COMPETITION

Engaging the Force can be advantageous;
Engaging the Force can be dangerous.

If the whole Force competes for advantage,
It will not be gained.
If caravans of the Force compete for advantage,
Transportation will be reduced significantly.

Although rolling up the defense
And hastening day and night without stopping
Will double the distance of a united movement,
Covering a hundred miles while competing for advantage
Will result in the capture of the Force's three leaders.
Those who are vigorous will be early,
And those who are tired will be late.
With this principle, only one in ten will arrive.

Covering fifty miles while competing for advantage
Will result in the fall of the Force's first leader.
With this principle, only half will arrive.

Covering thirty miles while competing for advantage
Will result in the arrival of only two of three divisions.

Therefore, a Force without significant transportation must lose;
One without provisions must lose;
One without supply caravans must lose.

The term *rolling up the defense* comes from an ideogram that refers to
a manuscript or painting that can be rolled up to transport or store.
Most early Chinese art and literature was produced in this portable scroll form.

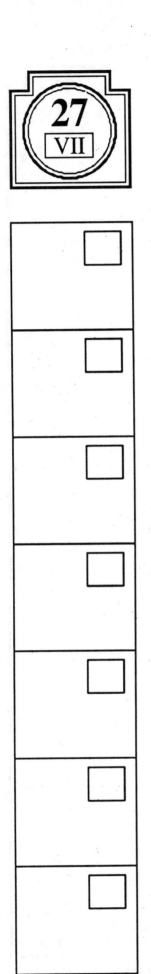

故不知諸侯之謀者，不能豫交。

不知山林險阻沮澤之形者，不能行軍。

不用鄉導者，不能得地利。

故兵以詐立，以利動，以分合爲變者也。

故其疾如風，其徐如林，侵掠如火，不動如山，

難知如陰，動如雷霆。

掠鄉分衆，廓地分利，懸權而動。

先知迂直之計者勝，此軍爭之法也。

FLEXIBILITY AND IMITATION

Those who do not know the Plan of other leaders
Are not able to prepare for negotiations.

Those who do not know the positions
Of the mountains, forests, passes, and marshes
Are not able to move the Force.

Those who do not employ local guides
Are not able to affect the Situation to advantage.

Imitation is basic to Strategy.
Move to follow the advantages.
Divide or unite to follow the Variations in action.

Hence, during swiftness, be like the wind.
During stillness, be like the forest.
During aggression, be like fire.
During immobility, be like a mountain.
Be as unknowable as the dark.
Move like a thunderbolt.

Take the region by distributing the numerous;
Open the territory by distributing the advantages.
Move with suspended flexibility.

Those who triumph
Know beforehand how to calculate the Direct and Indirect.
Such is Engaging the Force.

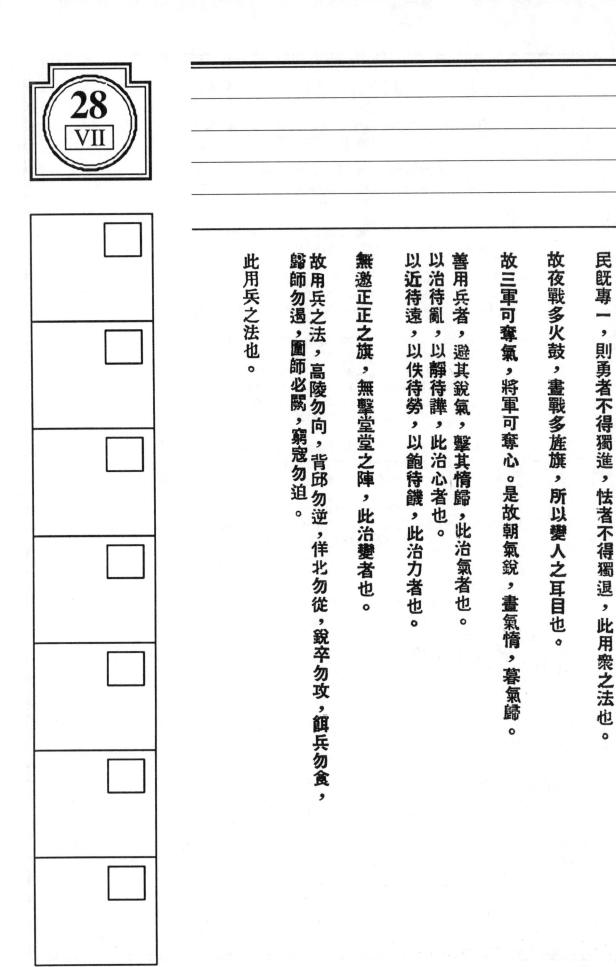

軍政曰：言不相聞，故爲鼓鐸；視不相見，故爲旌旗。

夫金鼓旌旗者，所以一民之耳目也。

民既專一，則勇者不得獨進，怯者不得獨退，此用衆之法也。

故夜戰多火鼓，晝戰多旌旗，所以變人之耳目也。

故三軍可奪氣，將軍可奪心。是故朝氣銳，晝氣惰，暮氣歸。

善用兵者，避其銳氣，擊其惰歸，此治氣者也。

以治待亂，以靜待譁，此治心者也。

以近待遠，以佚待勞，以飽待饑，此治力者也。

無邀正正之旗，無擊堂堂之陣，此治變者也。

故用兵之法，高陵勿向，背邱勿逆，佯北勿從，銳卒勿攻，餌兵勿食，歸師勿遏，圍師必闕，窮寇勿迫。

此用兵之法也。

CONTROLLING THE VARIATIONS

The *Chun Cheng* says: "When speakers cannot hear each other, act with drums and bells.
When observers cannot see each other, act with banners and flags.
In this way the eyes and ears of others are One
As they locate the gongs, drums, banners, and flags.
Once the focus of others is One,
Those who are bold will not advance alone; those who are fearful will not retreat alone.
Such is the Art of employing the numerous."

Thus, in nighttime challenges there should be many torches and drums;
In daytime challenges there should be many banners and flags.
In this way the eyes and ears of others can locate the Variations.

Now, an Entire Force can be robbed of its Spirit;
The Force's leaders can be robbed of their Composure.
In the morning the Spirit is sharp;
In the daytime the Spirit is idle;
At dusk the Spirit draws inward.

Hence, those skilled in the use of Strategy
Evade when the Spirit is sharp
And confront when the Spirit is idle or withdrawn —
Such is the way they control the Spirit.
The controlled lie in wait for the disorganized;
The calm lie in wait for the disorderly —
Such is the way they control Composure.
The near lie in wait for the distant;
The comfortable lie in wait for the troubled;
The satisfied lie in wait for the hungry —
Such is the way they control Strength.

They do not intercept when the banners are orderly and straightforward;
They never attack when the formation is impressive and imposing.
Such is the way they control the Variations.

Thus, to execute an Artful Strategy,
When the hill is high, never face up;
When the hill slopes behind, never back down;
When flight is feigned, never pursue;
When the other team is sharp, never attack;
When the Strategy is bait, never bite;
When the opposition withdraws, never interfere;
When surrounding the opposition, leave an opening;
When the opponent is desperate, never press.

Such is the execution of an Artful Strategy.

The *Chun Cheng* is an ancient military treatise, now lost.
It may be literally translated as "The Policies of the Military."

The word *Spirit* comes from the Chinese word *ch'i,* which can also be translated as "breath" or "character."
It refers to the inner strength and iife force of an individual.

The word *Composure* comes from the Chinese word *hsin,* which can be translated as
"heart," "mind," or "conscience." It refers to the true nature and higher mind of an individual.

C H A P T E R   E I G H T

THE NINE VARIATIONS

(SPONTANEITY IN THE FIELD)

$\mathcal{T}$HE NINE VARIATIONS IN TACTICS ARE BASED ON THE ADVANtages and disadvantages that occur during conflict as the strategy unfolds. Advantages give a strategy credibility, but the disadvantages of the opponent give the strategy its edge. Brilliant leaders have not only the ability to recognize their opponents' disadvantages — their disorder, confusion, weariness, lack of interest, unpreparedness, and miscalculations — but they are able to Vary the strategy to capitalize on them. Sun Tzu believed that once a challenge has been executed, skillful leaders must Vary their tactics. They must not allow a controlled strategy to inhibit creative counter-movement. Nor should commands from those at a distance interfere with spontaneous maneuvering in the immediate situation. "There are Rulers' orders that should not be accepted," said Sun Tzu. He insisted that one's tactics must change along with the situation and, furthermore, that some situations will develop that should not be confronted at all.

Sun Tzu warned that even if a leader has the skill and excellence to practice the Variations, there are character flaws common to leaders that can bring defeat. These flaws include recklessness, excessive caution, a short temper, fastidiousness, and deep personal attachments. He said: "The Five Weaknesses are a mistake in a leader. They are catastrophic in the execution of a Strategy. If a Force is defeated and a leader destroyed, it is certainly because of the Five Weaknesses."

CONFLICT IN THE SELF   After you confront an inner conflict, you must begin to Vary your normal pattern of behavior. You should not, however, become cautious and fearful, nor should you recklessly tempt your inner opponent. Both of these extremes are dangerous traps. Act confidently and stay on guard.

Your advantages — your determination, concentration, and creativity — are your weapons in overcoming inner conflicts. Use your advantages to expand your interests and focus your desires elsewhere. Do not linger in situations where the conflict is likely to surface. Your absence will begin to weaken your inner opponent.

Once you begin your challenge, your inner opponent will be watching and waiting for your guard to drop. You must, therefore, be alert. Sun Tzu said: "Rather than presuming they will not come, we lie in wait for their appearance. Rather than presuming they will not attack, we appear in a place they cannot attack."

CONFLICT IN THE ENVIRONMENT   In an environmental challenge, your strategy is only as good as your ability to act spontaneously.

Every new situation will require a Variation on your overall strategy. So whether you are stepping beyond family, neighborhood, work place, city, or country, be alert for situational tactics that can give you the advantage of surprise or illusion.

When you are transcending a difficult environment, guard against resentful, negative attitudes. They will block your progress. Keep your temper in check and your criticism to yourself, and develop some emotional indifference. Sun Tzu warned, "The quickly angered can be ridiculed. The very fastidious can be humiliated. The deeply attached can be harassed."

Once you have initiated an envirionmental challenge, you must take your own counsel, for you are unlikely to find support in your surroundings. You should now rely on your own strengths, and the weaknesses that you perceive in your environment, to show you the way. Your triumph over your environmental conflict will come through the clever use of these advantages and disadvantages.

CONFLICT WITH ANOTHER   During times of interpersonal conflict, execute your strategy in a timely manner in order to keep your opponent in motion. Use the changing circumstances of your interaction to trigger your tactical spontaneity. Each new maneuver that you initiate will further tax your opponent's strength and resources.

Use your own advantages — your clarity, your sense of destination, and your motivation — to rush your opponent's responses. Highlight your opponent's disadvantages — any confusion, misinformation, or uncertainty — to shake whatever composure your opponent has. This interplay of advantages and disadvantages will enhance the effectiveness of your strategy.

Especially, keep your emotions in check. Interpersonal conflicts are the most likely to undermine your self-control, and when that happens, you will make dangerous mistakes. Do not be fearful, boastful, angry, or vengeful. Direct indifference toward your opponent and focus only on your objectives and your strategy for achieving them.

CONFLICT AMONG LEADERS   Leaders carry a great responsibility, for they ultimately affect the destiny of both the organizations and the individuals involved. As the strategy unfolds, situations may develop that must be avoided rather than confronted. Many of the Variations that Sun Tzu described are "Paths that should not be taken." Leaders must be able to recognize these paths and redirect their forward momentum.

Skillful leaders continually evaluate their advantages and the disadvantages of their adversaries and incorporate these changing factors into their strategy. They use their own advantages — determination, confidence, thoroughness — to force their opponents to focus on their disadvantages: ennui, doubt, disorganization. This compromises the confidence of their opponents. Sun Tzu said: "Those who bend other leaders do so by means of disadvantages. Those who tax other leaders do so by means of activity. Those who hurry other leaders do so by means of advantages."

During interorganizational confrontations, a leader must remain in complete emotional control. Sun Tzu was emphatic about the severe damage that a leader's indulgences could bring to an organization. He warned: "The overly reckless can be destroyed. The overly cautious can be captured." Those leaders who are able to execute a successful strategy do so in a strictly professional manner.

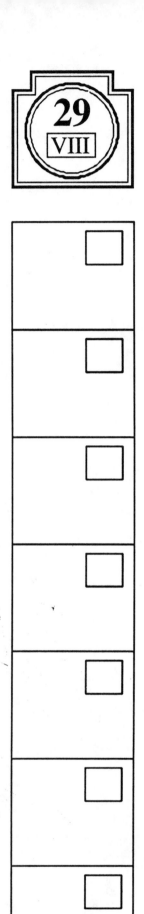

孫子曰：

凡用兵之法，將受命於君，合軍聚眾。

圯地無舍，衢地交合，絕地無留，圍地則謀，死地則戰。

途有所不由，軍有所不擊，城有所不攻，地有所不爭。

君命有所不受。

故將通於九變之利者，知用兵矣。

SITUATIONAL STRATEGIES

Sun Tzu said:

Generally, in executing an Artful Strategy,
The Leader is directed by a Ruler.
The Force is gathered and their numbers assembled.

In Obstructed Situations, do not take shelter.
In Intersecting Situations, gather to negotiate.
In Isolated Situations, do not linger.
In Surrounded Situations, there must be a scheme.
In Desperate Situations, there must be a challenge.

There are Paths that should not be taken.
There are Forces that should not be confronted.
There are Fortified Areas that should not be attacked.
There are Situations that should not be contested.

There are Rulers' orders that should not be accepted.

A Leader who understands the advantages in the Nine Variations
Knows how to execute a Strategy.

The word *Obstructed* comes from the ideogram for "bridge" or "riverbank."
In *The Art of Strategy*, it refers to an area that has limited possibilities for maneuvering or escape.

The "Ruler's orders that should not be accepted" is not one of The Nine Variations.
It is a summary statement pointing out that certain situations require a change in strategy.

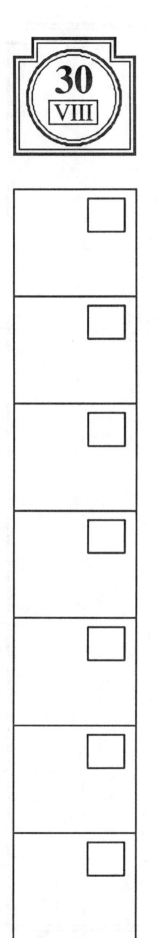

將不通於九變之利者，雖知地形，
不能得地之利矣。
治兵不知九變之術，雖知五利，
不能得人之用矣。
是故智者之慮，必雜於利害，
雜於利而務可信也，雜於害而患可解也。

COMBINING ADVANTAGES AND DISADVANTAGES

Leaders who do not understand the advantages of the Nine Variations,
Despite knowledge of the areas and positions,
Cannot gain advantage in the Situation.

In a controlled Strategy,
Those who do not know the theory of the Nine Variations,
Despite knowledge of the Five Advantages,
Cannot succeed in employing others.

Therefore, those who can speculate cleverly
Are certain to combine the advantages and the disadvantages.

With a combination of advantages,
The endeavor will have credibility;
With a combination of disadvantages,
Adversity can be overcome.

The *Five Advantages* that Sun Tzu mentions may be those outlined in Passage Twelve.
They are as follows: Knowing when and when not to challenge;
recognizing how to use the numerous and the few; agreeing on superior and inferior objectives;
preparing to wait for the unprepared; and leading without interference from a Ruler.

是故屈諸侯者以害。

役諸侯者以業。

趨諸侯者以利。

故用兵之法，

無恃其不來，恃吾有以待也。

無恃其不攻，恃吾有所不可攻也。

ANTICIPATING THE OPPONENT

Those who bend other leaders
Do so by means of disadvantages.

Those who tax other leaders
Do so by means of activity.

Those who hurry other leaders
Do so by means of advantages.

Thus, in executing an Artful Strategy,

Rather than presuming they will not come,
We lie in wait for their appearance.

Rather than presuming they will not attack,
We appear in a place they cannot attack.

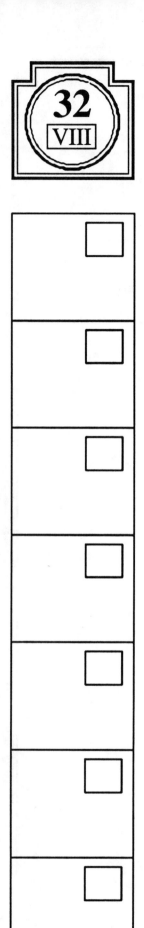

故將有五危：

必死，可殺也；必生，可虜也；忿速，可侮也；廉潔，可辱也；愛民，可煩也。

凡此五者，將之過也，用兵之災也。

覆軍殺將，必以五危。

不可不察也。

FIVE WEAKNESSES IN LEADERS

Leaders may have Five Weaknesses:

The overly reckless can be destroyed.
The overly cautious can be captured.
The quickly angered can be ridiculed.
The very fastidious can be humiliated.
The deeply attached can be harassed.

Generally, the Five Weaknesses are a mistake in a leader.
They are catastrophic in the execution of a Strategy.

If a Force is defeated and a leader destroyed,
It is certainly because of the Five Weaknesses.

These must be carefully studied.

C H A P T E R   N I N E

MOVING THE FORCE

(CONFRONTATION IN THE FIELD)

*W*HEN SKILLFUL LEADERS MUST ENTER INTO A CONFRONTA- tion, they are chiefly concerned with optimizing and protecting their own Force — their strategy, resources, and advantages — and evaluating and anticipating their opponents' Force. Every confrontation has its own terrain, or situation, which Sun Tzu classified into four types: mountains, water- ways, marshes, and level ground. He believed that leaders must have the ability to Move and position their Force through any situation, while max- imizing both their security and their field of opportunity. Sun Tzu said: "When security is cultivated and the position is Realistic, the Force will remain healthy and can assume certain triumph. In this way, the Situation helps bring advantage to the Strategy."

Once the situation is known and strategic accommodations are made, skillful leaders focus attention on the conduct of their opponents in order to discover their rival's position, strengths, vulnerabilities, and strategy. Through careful observation at the start of confrontation, aware leaders are able to obtain significant intelligence about their opponents. They can discover their opponents' assessment of the situation, and learn whether they plan an ultimate advance or retreat. They can discover whether their opponents have a pressing deadline, or if they are disorganized or in dis- tress. Such strategic information will show a superior leader the way to certain triumph.

CONFLICT IN THE SELF   The most difficult challenge during an inner confrontation is to maintain a constant guard against your inner oppo- nent. Your inner opponent is a part of your consciousness, which is its great advantage. Therefore you must protect your determination — your Moving Force — by avoiding areas where your inner opponent can gain the upper hand. Sun Tzu said: "Situations where there are isolating gorges or natural hollows, cages, snares, traps, and crevices must be left quickly or never approached."

On the other hand, you have a strong advantage over your inner oppo- nent: You are able to constantly monitor its strength and position, and use this knowledge to position yourself well and your inner opponent poorly. The one who is held in a poor position — exposed and undersupplied — is the one who is inevitably defeated.

Your personal growth, beyond this or any other conflict, depends on your level of self-control. Self-discipline will naturally develop out of any determined challenge of an inner conflict. By cultivating self-discipline, you will find that you can accomplish more and more in life with greater ease and success.

CONFLICT IN THE ENVIRONMENT   Your Force in environmen- tal conflicts is your determination, your growing detachment, and your sense of ultimate destination. As you mobilize yourself into a position for personal triumph, you must carefully protect your resources. You will need them later, for new beginnings.

Sun Tzu described four type of environments and suggested the best way to Move the Force through them. Among mountains, Move through the valleys and low areas to avoid attention; rest in high areas for security and perspective. At waterways, cross if you must, then Move away; do not get swept up by current events. In marshes, as in any sticky area, Move quickly and lightly to avoid getting stuck. On exposed level ground, keep your face toward your conflict and safety at your back.

Your environment is as much a part of you as you are a part of your environment. Use this intimacy to observe and evaluate its rhythms and attitudes, its fears and hidden safeguards. Your knowledge of your environment is your ultimate guarantee of a successful transition.

CONFLICT WITH ANOTHER   Interpersonal confrontations can produce the most intense emotional states. You must control strong feelings, however, if your strategy is to unfold successfully. Sublimate your emotions by directing your energies toward evaluating your opponent. "In an intense Strategy," said Sun Tzu, "where one may face the other for a long time without engaging and without retreating, careful observations are essential."

As you observe, try to determine your opponent's strengths, fears, vulnerabilities, and plan of attack. All of these are revealed to an experienced observer at the time of interpersonal confrontation. Then, alter your position to remain outside the range of attack; and alter your strategy to throw your opponent off guard. This is Moving the Force.

Interpersonal confrontations generally come about when negotiations are unfeasible and acquiesence to your opponent will compromise your growth. Confrontations permanently alter relationships, despite whatever compromise or resolution is reached. Therefore, be certain of your determination before you confront, and prepare for your relationship to take a very different form.

CONFLICT AMONG LEADERS   Interorganizational confrontations generally occur in a terrain or area outside of either organization. This area — be it a battlefield, a courtroom, or a marketplace — has its own structures, systems, and hazards. Therefore, during confrontation, leaders must focus on three elements simultaneously: their strategy, their opponent, and Moving their Force safely through uncertain terrain.

Every skilled leader knows that the time of confrontation is the best opportunity to evaluate their adversaries. Careful observations will reveal their opponents' strengths and, most importantly, signs of their distress. An opponent's disorganization, deadlines, desperation, or uncertainties are formidable weapons in the hands of a superior strategist.

The aim of every leader during times of interorganizational confrontation is to maintain coordination, cooperation, and commitment among all members of the organization. These come about through qualities of leadership that are met with heartfelt respect, and are maintained through a well-structured system of penalty and reward. Sun Tzu insisted that commitment is cultivated through superior leadership. He said: "Those who can set forth commands with absolute credibility can bring the numerous together in success."

孫子曰：凡處軍相敵。

絕山依谷，視生處高，戰隆無登，此處山之軍也。

絕水必遠水，客絕水而來，勿迎之於水內，令半渡而擊之，利。欲戰者，無附於水而迎客，視生處高，無迎水流，此處水上之軍也。

絕斥澤，惟亟去無留，若交軍於斥澤之中，必依水草，而背眾樹，此處斥澤之軍也。

平陸處易，而右背高，前死後生，此處平陸之軍也。

凡此四軍之利，黃帝之所以勝四帝也。

凡軍喜高而惡下，貴陽而賤陰，養生而處實，軍無百疾，是謂必勝。

丘陵隄防，必處其陽，而右背之，此兵之利，地之助也。

上雨，水沫至，欲涉者，待其定也。

凡地有絕澗，天井，天牢，天羅，天陷，天隙，必亟去之，勿近也。吾遠之，敵近之；吾迎之，敵背之。

USING THE SITUATION

Sun Tzu said:
Generally, when positioning the Force and evaluating the opponent,

Cross mountains by following the valleys.
Find security in the higher positions.
Do not climb up in order to challenge.
Such is the position of the Force among mountains.

Cross waterways and keep them at a distance.
If adventurers cross the water in order to approach, never meet them midstream.
The danger caused them in crossing for confrontation is itself an advantage.
Those who wish to challenge should not be near water when facing adventurers.
They find security in the higher positions; they do not meet in flowing water.
Such is the ideal position of the Force among waterways.

Cross marshes concerned only with leaving them and not lingering.
If the Force is engaged in the midst of a marsh,
Hold to the grassy banks, backed against the trees.
Such is the position of the Force in the marsh.

Level ground is easy to occupy.
Put heights behind and to the right,
So that danger is in front and the rear is secure.
Such is the position of the Force on level ground.

Generally, it is these Four that will bring advantage to the Force.
It was these Four that gave the Yellow Emperor excellence among emperors.

Ordinarily, the Force prefers heights and hates the lowlands;
It treasures the light and disdains the darkness.
When security is cultivated and the position is Realistic,
The Force will remain healthy and can assume certain triumph.
So in areas of hills and embankments,
Occupy a position in the light, sloping up behind, and to the right.
In this way the Situation helps bring advantage to the Strategy.

When there is rain above and waterways are flooded,
Those who wish to cross should wait for it to subside.

Generally, Situations where there are isolating gorges
Or natural hollows, cages, snares, traps, and crevices
Must be left quickly or never approached.
We keep away from these to direct the opponent near them.
We face these so that they are at the opponent's back.

The Yellow Emperor, Huang Ti, was a legendary ruler of China,
believed to have reigned from 2698 to 2598 B.C.

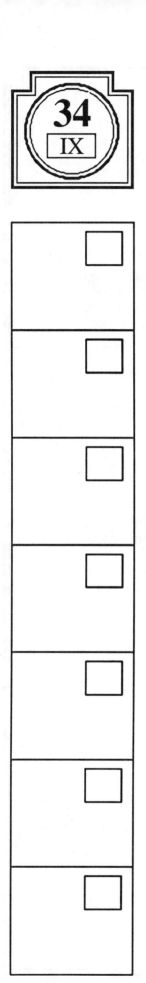

軍旁有險阻蔣潢，井生葭葦，山林蘙薈，必謹覆索之，此伏奸之所藏也。

敵近而靜者，恃其險也；遠而挑戰者，欲人之進也；其所居易者，利也。

眾樹動者，來也；眾草多障者，疑也；鳥起者，伏也；獸駭者，覆也。

塵高而銳者，車來也；卑而廣者，徒來也；散而條達者，樵採也；少而往來者，營軍也。

辭卑而益備者，進也；辭強而進驅者，退也；輕車先出居其側者，陳也。

無約而請和者，謀也；奔走而陳兵者，期也；半進半退者，誘也。

DETERMINING THE OPPONENT'S STRATEGY

When the Force is adjacent to strategic passes,
Or ponds and hollows overgrown with rushes and reeds,
Or mountain forests screened with luxuriant growth,
These must be carefully and repeatedly examined.
They may be an adversary's location for ambush or place of concealment.

Opponents who are near and yet calm presume they are formidable.
Those who are distant and yet provoking want others to advance.
Those who occupy an accessible location believe they have the advantage.

Those who are approaching move among the forest trees.
Those who are doubtful screen themselves behind the tall grasses.
Those who are lying in ambush cause birds to rise in flight.
Those who are in sudden advance cause animals to start.

Those who are approaching with vehicles raise tall swirling dust clouds.
Those who are approaching on foot raise low wide dust clouds.
Those who are collecting fuel raise regular scattered dust clouds.
Those who are encamping their corps raise small circulating dust clouds.

Those who are about to advance speak humbly and yet increase their preparations.
Those who are about to retreat speak evasively and yet push provocatively.
Those who are about to deploy send out light vehicles early to occupy the flanks.

Those who are executing a scheme call for a truce without proposing an agreement.
Those who have reached their deadline deploy their strategy with hurried movements.
Those who are attempting to entice partially advance and partially retreat.

倚仗而立者，饑也；汲而先飲者，渴也；見利而不進者，勞也。

鳥集者，虛也；夜呼者，恐也；軍擾者，將不重也；旌旗動者，亂也；吏怒者，倦也。

粟馬肉食，軍無懸瓿，不返其舍者，窮寇也；諄諄翕翕，徐言入入者，失眾也。

廪賞者，窘也；數罰者，困也。先暴而後畏其眾者，不精之至也；來委謝者，欲休息也。

兵怒而相迎，久而不合，又不解去，必謹察之。

兵非益多也，惟無武進，足以併力料敵，取人而已。

夫惟無慮而易敵者，必擒於人。

DETERMINING THE OPPONENT'S VULNERABILITY

Those who stand using their weapons for support are hungry.
Those whose water carriers drink first are thirsty.
Those who see an advantage but do not advance are troubled.

Wherever birds gather it is deserted.
Those who are clamorous at night are fearful.
Those who have desertion in their corps have leaders without significance.
Those who move their banners and flags about are disorganized.
Those whose officers are easily angered are tired.

The horses feed on grains and the corps on meat.
Opponents who do not hang their cooking pot
Or return to their shelter are desperate.
Those who continually gather in closed groups,
Whispering and murmuring speculations, sense numerous losses.

Those who are hard-pressed have repeated rewards.
Those who are in distress have frequent penalties.
Those who are extremely unrefined
Are initially ferocious and later fearful of others' numbers.
Those who long to take a rest send generous messages.

In an intense Strategy,
Where one may face the other for a long time
Without engaging and without retreating,
Careful observations are essential.

A Strategy is not enhanced by numbers.
An advantage comes not merely by force.
It is enough to foresee and match the opponents' strength,
To take hold of them and end it.

Those who think that their opponents are easy
Without making careful calculations,
Are certain to be captured by them.

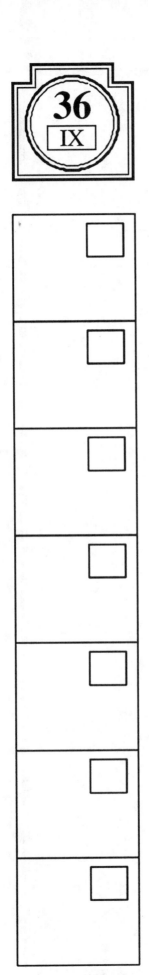

卒未親附而罰之，則不服，不服則難用也。

卒已親附，而罰不行，則不可用也。

故令之以文，齊之以武，是謂必取。

令素行以教其民，則民服。

令不素行，以教其民，則民不服。

令素信著者，與眾相得也。

THE CULTIVATION OF ALLEGIANCE

If the team does not yet feel a strong commitment,
They will not obey when they are penalized.
Employment without obedience will result in trouble.

If the team already feels a strong commitment
And yet penalties are not imposed,
Employment will still be ineffective.

Thus, commands that come through cultivation
Can equal those that come through force.
This is known as an accomplishment.

Commands that are straightforward
Will enlighten others and result in their obedience.

Commands that are not straightforward
Will not enlighten others or bring their obedience.

Those who can set forth commands with absolute credibility
Can bring the numerous together in success.

CHAPTER TEN

SITUATIONAL POSITIONING

(POSITIONING DURING CONFRONTATION)

*A*T A TIME OF CONFRONTATION, SITUATIONAL POSITIONING IS A skillful leader's most formidable strategic maneuver. Sun Tzu believed that every Situation and its potential transformations could be analyzed so that clever Positioning would capture the advantage. He described the Six Positions that may be dictated by any Situation — smooth, entangled, indecisive, narrow, obstructed, and distant — and explained tactical maneuvers appropriate to each. He said: "These Six are the Tao of Situations. It is a leader's greatest duty to study them carefully."

Sun Tzu emphasized the importance of superior leadership during a confrontation. Brilliant leaders make certain that every action results in advantage for the strategy and protection for the Force. Such leaders do not seek fame or recognition, nor do they fear blame or retribution. They advance only when victory is clear, and they retreat immediately if the Force is jeopardized. Sun Tzu called this style of leadership "a treasure for the Organization." It is the ability to evaluate the opponent that tells a superior leader when to confront; but it is Situational Positioning that makes the confrontation so devastating. Sun Tzu pointed out: "Know the other and know yourself: Triumph without peril. Know Nature and know the Situation: Triumph completely."

CONFLICT IN THE SELF   Regardless of your sense of urgency or distaste for your inner opponent, do not confront an inner conflict when you are weak or uncertain. The key to victory over inner conflicts is to challenge them only when you are certain of triumph. Therefore, time your strategic offensive for the moment when your Position is at its strongest and most fully supported.

Generally, during an inner confrontation your Position will be what Sun Tzu called Smooth. In a Smooth Position, you have direct access to your inner opponent, and vice versa. The ideal strategy in this Position is to put yourself between your inner opponent and its support system. Then block the supplies and withdraw the energy by directing your interests and desires elsewhere.

The greatest danger to your strategy during an inner confrontation is what Sun Tzu called Disorder. Disorder brings defeat and can be caused by any of four flaws: discipline that is lax or nonexistent; objectives that are fundamentally wrong; tactics that are unprincipled (the ends do not justify the means); or a strategy that is overly indulgent or overly restrictive. Guard against these flaws and triumph can be yours.

CONFLICT IN THE ENVIRONMENT   Situational Positioning is essential to survival during an environmental confrontation. An environment may hold all of the Situational Positions that Sun Tzu described — smooth, entangled, indecisive, narrow, obstructed, and distant — and each Position can block your progress. In order to transcend your environment or to reform your relationship to it, you must Situate yourself cleverly within the Positions where you find yourself.

A direct confrontation with your environment should not be mounted until you are beyond its traps. Do not challenge your environment unless you are emotionally and financially disengaged from it, and confident of your ultimate triumph. If you are uncertain of victory, it is because you have not been thorough in your planning and are unclear about your ultimate destination.

The foundation of a winning strategy during an environmental confrontation is a careful understanding of your Position. Sun Tzu said: "A superior leader who follows the Tao... calculates the distance or proximity of dangers and obstructions." When you can move with confidence anywhere in your environment, you are on the path to triumph.

CONFLICT WITH ANOTHER   Interpersonal confrontations are extremely stressful, but you must not succumb to anxiety. In fact, any emotional reaction at all is an indulgence that can stand in the way of your success. Now is the time to employ all of your analytical skills, for they are your most reliable guidelines during a highly charged confrontation.

By the time you have prepared yourself to mount an interpersonal confrontation, you should have a deep understanding of your opponent's strengths, fears, and likely responses. In addition, you should thoroughly understand yourself — your determination, motivations, and objectives. Knowing your opponent and knowing yourself are Sun Tzu's first essentials of triumph.

Finally, to assure your victory, you must be able to recognize the relative Positions of yourself and your opponent. Any of the Six Positions that Sun Tzu outlined can occur during interpersonal confrontations. You should know how to precisely Position yourself in each Situation in order to capture the advantage. Sun Tzu believed that if you know yourself and your opponent, as well as Situational Positioning, you are certain to "triumph completely."

CONFLICT AMONG LEADERS   At the time of interorganizational confrontation, superior leaders are chiefly concerned with protecting their team. If they perceive that the team might be jeopardized, they do not confront their opponents, regardless of any outstanding imperatives. Sun Tzu said of brilliant leaders: "To advance without seeking fame or to retreat without avoiding blame... is a treasure for the Organization."

Sun Tzu described Six Mistakes that a leader may make as teams are formed and strategies are executed: A confrontation with a much larger team results in Flight; weak officers result in Insubordination; a weak team results in Collapse; resentful officers result in Disintegration; unprincipled officers result in Disorder; an unfocused strategy results in Desertion. Sun Tzu explained: "These Six are the Tao of defeat. It is the leader's greatest duty to study them carefully."

A leader who does not know how to Position the team for advantage in any Situation will face defeat, regardless of how powerful or large the organization. Interorganizational confrontations are subject to each of the Six Situational Positions for which Sun Tzu presented guidelines: Challenge when the Position is Smooth; do not challenge when the Position is Entangled; confront when the Position is Indecisive; pursue only if a Narrow Position is empty; occupy or empty an Obstructed Position; do not challenge from a Distant Position. Those who know Situational Positioning, said Sun Tzu, "move without delusion and progress without tiring."

孫子曰：

地形有通者，有挂者，有支者，有隘者，有險者，有遠者。

我可以往，彼可以來，曰通；通形者，先居高陽，利糧道，以戰則利。

可以往，難以返，曰挂；挂形者，敵無備，出而勝之；敵若有備，出而不勝，難以返，不利。

我出而不利，彼出而不利，曰支；支形者，敵雖利我，我無出也；引而去，令敵半出而擊之，利。

隘形者，我先居之，必盈之以待敵；若敵先居之，盈而勿從，不盈而從之。

險形者，我先居之，必居高陽以待敵；若敵先居之，引而去之，勿從也。

遠形者，勢均難以挑戰，戰而不利。

凡此六者，地之道也，將之至任，不可不察也。

THE SIX POSITIONS

Sun Tzu said:

Among Situational Positions,
There are those that are Smooth,
Those that are Entangled,
Those that are Indecisive,
Those that are Narrow,
Those that are Obstructed,
Those that are Distant.

Smooth means we can go forward and others can approach.
In a Smooth Position,
Those who are first to occupy the heights and the light
Have an advantage over the path of provisions.
A challenge then will be advantageous.

Entangled means we can go forward but will have difficulty returning.
In an Entangled Position,
If the opponent is unprepared, those who move first will triumph.
If the opponent seems prepared, those who move first will not triumph.
Since it is difficult to return, there is no advantage.

Indecisive means neither we nor others can move first advantageously.
In a Indecisive Position,
Despite any advantage over the opponent, we do not move first.
We lure with a retreat, causing the opponent to partially retreat.
A confrontation then will be advantageous.

In a Narrow Position,
We must be first to occupy it fully and lie in wait for the opponent.
When the opponent is first to occupy it,
Never pursue if they fill it; pursue only if it is not yet full.

In an Obstructed Position,
We must be first to occupy the heights and the light to await the opponent.
When the opponent is first to occupy these,
We never pursue; we lure with a retreat.

In a Distant Position, both forces are equal.
Because here it is difficult to provoke a challenge,
A challenge will not be advantageous.

Generally, these Six are the Tao of Situations.
It is a leader's greatest duty to study them carefully.

The word *light* comes from the Chinese word *yang*, as in *yin-yang*.
It can also be translated as "positive," "sun," or "bright."
In *The Art of Strategy*, it refers to the advantageous position where the sun is at one's back.

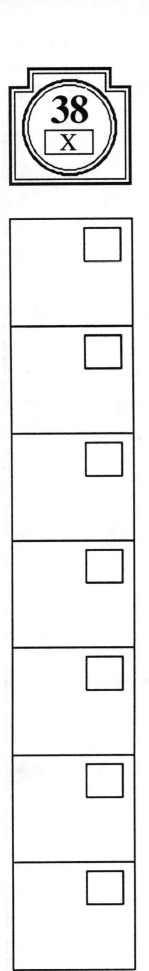

故兵有走者，有弛者，有陷者，有崩者，有亂者，有北者。

凡此六種，非天之災，將之過也。

夫勢均，以一擊十，曰走。

卒強吏弱，曰弛。

吏強卒弱，曰陷。

大吏怒而不服，遇敵懟而自戰，將不知其能，曰崩。

將弱不嚴，敎道不明，吏卒無常，陳兵縱橫，曰亂。

將不能料敵，以少合眾，以弱擊強，兵無選鋒，曰北。

凡此六者，敗之道也，將之至任，不可不察也。

THE SIX STRATEGIC MISTAKES

Among Strategies,
There are those that result in Flight,
Those that result in Insubordination,
Those that result in Collapse,
Those that result in Disintegration,
Those that result in Disorder,
Those that result in Desertion.

Generally, these Six come not from natural catastrophes,
But from the mistakes of leaders.

Flight means:
Other conditions being equal, one confronts another ten times more powerful.

Insubordination means:
The team is strong and the officers are weak.

Collapse means:
The officers are strong and the team is weak.

Disintegration means:
The senior officers are angry and defiant.
They meet the opponent hatefully and challenge on their own behalf,
Without the knowledge of the leader.

Disorder means:
The leader is weak and undisciplined.
The philosophy is not enlightened by the Tao.
The officers and team have no principles.
The Strategy is deployed indulgently and illogically.

Desertion means:
The leader is unable to evaluate the opponent,
So the few engage the numerous
And the weak confront the strong;
The Strategy is flat and unfocused.

Generally, these Six are the Tao of defeat.
It is the leader's greatest duty to study them carefully.

夫地形者，兵之助也。

料敵制勝，計險阨遠近，上將之道也。

知此而用戰者，必勝；不知此而用戰者，必敗。

故戰道必勝，主曰無戰，必戰可也；

戰道不勝，主曰必戰，無戰可也。

故進不求名，退不避罪，唯民是保，而利合於主，國之寶也。

SUPERIOR LEADERSHIP

Situational Positioning is an aid to Strategy.

A Superior Leader who follows the Tao
Evaluates the opponent's formula for triumph
And calculates the distance or proximity of dangers and obstructions.

Those who employ this knowledge
Can challenge with the certainty of triumph.
Those who do not employ this knowledge
Can challenge with the certainty of defeat.

Thus, if the View calls for no challenge,
Yet the Tao of challenge is certain triumph,
Then a challenge must be made.

If the View calls for challenge,
Yet the Tao of challenge is certain defeat,
Then a challenge must not be made.

Therefore, to advance without seeking fame
Or to retreat without avoiding blame
Will bring security to the People and advantage to the View.
This is a treasure for the Organization.

The word *View* here, as in Passage One, is from the ideogram that refers to
a sovereign or to the official policies of state.

視卒如嬰兒，故可與之赴深谿；視卒如愛子，故可與之俱死。

厚而不能使，愛而不能令，亂而不能治，譬如驕子，不可用也。

知吾卒之可以擊，而不知敵之不可擊，勝之半也。

知敵之可擊，而不知吾卒之不可以擊，勝之半也。

知敵之可擊，知吾卒之可以擊，而不知地形之不可以戰，勝之半也。

故知兵者，動而不迷，舉而不窮。

故曰：知彼知己，勝乃不殆；知地知天，勝乃可全。

KNOWING THE SITUATION

Regard the team as children and they will go into the deepest valleys.
Regard the team as offspring and they will share the ultimate dangers.

The indulged cannot be made useful;
The favored cannot be directed;
The disorderly cannot be controlled.
Like spoiled children, they cannot be employed.

If we know our team is able to confront,
But do not know if the opponent is vulnerable,
We are but halfway to triumph.

If we know the opponent is able to confront,
But do not know if our team is vulnerable,
We are but halfway to triumph.

If we know the opponent is able to confront
And know our team is able to confront,
But do not know Situational Positioning,
We are unable to challenge
Because we are still but halfway to triumph.

Thus, those who understand Strategy
Move without delusion and progress without tiring.

Hence the saying:
"Know the other and know yourself:
Triumph without peril.
Know Nature and know the Situation:
Triumph completely."

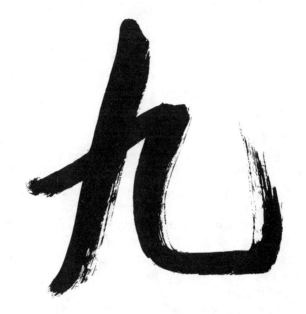

CHAPTER ELEVEN

THE NINE SITUATIONS

(MOBILIZING DURING CONFRONTATION)

$\mathcal{U}$P TO THIS POINT, SUN TZU'S DISCUSSIONS IN *THE ART OF Strategy* have been both a preparation for and a deterrent to open confrontation. Should confrontation actually erupt, the Nine Situations are Sun Tzu's strategy for mobilizing the Force. Sun Tzu described Nine classic Situations that determine the nature of any confrontation, and for each he explained deployments a leader may use in order to gain advantage over the opponent. During mobilization the skills of superior leadership are most critical: Leaders must act on their instincts, for there is no time for consideration; they must rely on their experience, for there is no time for consultation.

Sun Tzu also outlined a general strategy to press the opponent into further disadvantage. Superior leaders continually seek to prevent unity among their opponents by blocking opportunities for gatherings and agreements. Sun Tzu said: "The Strategy of the Superior Leader is to thwart a large organization so that their numbers cannot grow; and to inspire awe among their opponents so that their meetings do not unify." Brilliant leaders also pinpoint their opponents' weakness by discovering their greatest attachments or expectations. "Locate beforehand his deepest attachment and then seize it. He will comply!" said Sun Tzu. "Feign acceptance of the opponent's objectives, then turn on the opponent as One. Even from a thousand miles away the command can be destroyed." Throughout, an ingenious leader will unfold the strategy at full speed to intimidate the opponent, and will protect those involved from harm.

CONFLICT IN THE SELF   When you actively confront your inner opponent, you must act quickly and decisively. Throw yourself into Situations that spark your awareness and strengthen your determination. Sun Tzu said: "Speed presides over the conditions of strategy. Seize opportunities so that others do not gain. Take paths that are unexpected and attack locations that are unprotected."

"When a swift challenge is necessary for survival because a delayed challenge results in extinction," Sun Tzu said, "the Situation is Desperate." Because inner confrontations occur in an intimate and closed system, they can create a Desperate Situation. When your health or happiness depends absolutely on your complete triumph over an inner opponent, the Situation is Desperate.

Once you are in the midst of your struggle, never indulge in self-doubt. Your inner opponent's greatest advantage is your lack of belief in your ultimate triumph. Do not allow yourself to even visualize a retreat or respite from your struggle. Sun Tzu pointed out: "Those who are in a Desperate Situation must press onward without a location."

CONFLICT IN THE ENVIRONMENT   In an environmental confrontation, you must act decisively and make certain that your reinforcements are in place. Because triumph is generally won by the contender who takes the first advantage, environmental confrontations are what Sun Tzu described as Competitive Situations. He said: "When either we or others must seize the advantage, the Situation is Competitive.... In Competitive Situations, we lead by hurrying our backups."

Any open confrontation with your environment must be resolved rapidly and without delay. An environment has tremendous endurance and resistance, while your own energy is finite. Therefore, make certain that your strategy remains invisible until the moment it is unleashed. In this way you will capture the first advantage. Sun Tzu said: "Follow the rules and accommodate the opponent, all the while Working toward the decisive challenge."

After a confrontation has been initiated, you must go forward without rest until your conflict is settled. If you are unable to restructure your environment, it will be necessary for you to free yourself from it immediately. Remember, the objective in an environmental confrontation is to reposition yourself in your world in order to achieve personal fulfillment.

CONFLICT WITH ANOTHER   To gain the advantage in an interpersonal confrontation, it is important to locate beforehand your opponent's deepest desire or attachment. This is your opponent's vulnerability. When this vulnerability is successfully threatened, your opponent will be forced to yield.

Do not, however, attempt to intimidate your opponent by describing your plan of attack. Sun Tzu believed that it is far more intimidating to execute a decisive strategy that others can neither analyze nor anticipate. He said of such clever strategists: "They alter the Work and adjust the Plan so that others cannot discern; they alter the position and detour the route so that others cannot calculate."

A confrontation with another can involve any of the Nine Situations that Sun Tzu described. Whatever the Situation, you must respond accurately until the confrontation is concluded. Stay alert for the first opportunity to capture the advantage. "Then," said Sun Tzu, "act in a flash so the opponent is unable to resist."

CONFLICT AMONG LEADERS   When a leader brings an organization into a direct and open confrontation with a rival organization, it is a Situation of grave significance. Because the fates of so many are involved in the outcome, a leader must possess extraordinary skill and demonstrate brilliance in strategic awareness. If this is not the case, confrontation can be catastrophic.

During confrontation, superior leaders strive to divide their opponents and separate their factions. Sun Tzu said, "Those whom the Ancient Ones called skilled in the Execution of Strategy make it impossible for their opponents' advance and backup to reach each other, for their numerous and few to rely on each other, for their talented and inexperienced to rescue each other, for their superior and inferior to protect each other."

At the same time, skilled leaders strive to maintain absolute unity in their own organization. They know that the key to victory is unity within the team, and if failure occurs, it comes through a loss of connection and team spirit. Therefore, they keep the organization unified by overriding bureaucratic policies and by rewarding members generously.

孫子曰：用兵之法，有散地，有輕地，有爭地，有交地，有衢地，有重地，有圮地，有圍地，有死地。

諸侯自戰其地，為散地；入人之地，而不深者，為輕地；我得則利，彼得亦利者，為爭地；我可以往，彼可以來者，為交地；諸侯之地三屬，先至而得天下之眾者，為衢地；入人之地深，背城邑多者，為重地；行山林、險阻、沮澤，凡難行之道者，為圮地；所由入者隘，所從歸者迂，彼寡可以擊吾之眾者，為圍地；疾戰則存，不疾戰則亡者，為死地。

是故散地則無以戰，輕地則無止，爭地則無攻，交地則無絕，衢地則合交，重地則掠，圮地則行，圍地則謀，死地則戰。

所謂古之善用兵者，能使敵人前後不相及，眾寡不相恃，貴賤不相救，上下不相扶。

卒離而不集，兵合而不齊。合於利而動，不合於利而止。

敢問：敵眾整而將來，待之若何？曰：先奪其所愛，則聽矣。

兵之情主速，乘人之不及，由不虞之道，攻其所不戒也。

SITUATIONAL RESPONSE

Sun Tzu said: In executing an Artful Strategy, there are Situations that are
Idle, Simple, Competitive, Negotiable, Intersecting, Serious,
Obstructed, Surrounded, and Desperate.

When other leaders challenge from their own territory,
The Situation is Idle.
When others approach but have not yet penetrated the territory,
The Situation is Simple.
When either we or others must seize the advantage,
The Situation is Competitive.
When we can go forward and others can approach,
The Situation is Negotiable.
When the first one to reach the dependent domains
Can affect the Entire System and its multitudes,
The Situation is Intersecting.
When others approach and penetrate the territory
With many fortifications behind them,
The Situation is Serious.
When the path runs through mountains, forests, passes, or marshes
Where the way is generally difficult,
The Situation is Obstructed.
When the approach to a location is narrow and the return is circuitous,
And a small number of others can confront our larger numbers,
The Situation is Surrounded.
When a swift challenge is necessary for survival
Because a delayed challenge results in extinction,
The Situation is Desperate.

Hence, in an Idle Situation, challenge not; in a Simple Situation, rest not.
In a Competitive Situation, attack not; in a Negotiating Situation, cease not.
In an Intersecting Situation, gather and negotiate.
In a Serious Situation, seize; in an Obstructed Situation, move.
In a Surrounded Situation, scheme; in a Desperate Situation, challenge.

Those whom the Ancient Ones called
Skilled in the Execution of Strategy make it impossible
For their opponents' advance and backup to reach each other,
For their numerous and few to rely on each other,
For their talented and inexperienced to rescue each other,
For their superior and inferior to protect each other.

A team that is separated cannot gather, and their unified strategy cannot unfold.
With unity it is advantageous to move; without unity it is advantageous to stop.

Venture to ask: "What if an opposing leader approaches
With his multitudes whole and ready?"
I say: "Locate beforehand his deepest attachment and then seize it. He will comply!"

Speed presides over the conditions of strategy.
Seize opportunities so that others do not gain.
Take paths that are unexpected, and attack locations that are unprotected.

凡為客之道，深入則專，主人不克，掠於饒野，三軍足食，謹養而勿勞，併氣積力，運兵計謀，為不可測。投之無所往，死且不北。

死焉不得士人盡力？兵士甚陷則不懼，無所往則固，深入則拘，不得已則鬥。是故其兵不修而戒，不求而得，不約而親，不令而信。

禁祥去疑，至死無所之。吾士無餘財，非惡貨也；無餘命，非惡壽也。令發之日，士卒坐者涕沾襟，偃臥者涕交頤，投之無所往者，諸劌之勇也。

故善用兵，譬如率然。率然者，常山之蛇也。擊其首，則尾至；擊其尾，則首至；擊其中，則首尾俱至。敢問：兵可使如率然乎？曰：可。夫吳人與越人相惡也，當其同舟而濟遇風，其相救也，如左右手。

是故方馬埋輪，未足恃也；齊勇若一，政之道也；剛柔皆得，地之理也。

故善用兵者，携手若使一人，不得已也。

將軍之事，靜以幽，正以治；能愚士卒之耳目，使之無知。易其事，革其謀，使人無識；易其居，迂其途，使人不得慮。

帥與之期，如登高而去其梯；帥與之深入諸侯之地，而發其機。焚舟破釜，若驅羣羊，驅而往，驅而來，莫知所之。聚三軍之眾，投之於險，此謂將軍之事也。

THE SPIRIT OF THE CORPS

Generally, it is the Tao of Adventurers
To focus as they approach and penetrate, so the View is not overcome;
To forage in the abundant countryside, so the Entire Force has enough food;
To carefully train to avoid anxiety, so their strength of Spirit merges and accumulates;
To rotate their Strategy of Calculated Plans, so their actions cannot be measured;
To take no location but thrust ever onward, so they may meet danger without desertion.

Why are they not endangered when they exhaust their strength to overtake the other corps?
They lose their fear when the Strategy of others is to harm them.
They grow determined when compelled onward without location.
They become controlled when they must penetrate deeply.
They will fight when there is no gain in stopping.
Hence, the Strategy is, protection without forethought; attainment without asking;
Commitment without contracts; trust without orders.

Prohibit omens and discard doubt, so desperation will not find a place.
It is not because they disdain resources that our corps is without excess wealth.
It is not because they disdain longevity that they are without excess life.
The day the team is ordered to start out,
Those sitting may wet their collars with tears; those reclining may wet their cheeks with tears.
But those who thrust onward without a location will have the courage of Chu and Kuei.

Hence, those skilled in the execution of a Strategy
Are like the *shuai jan* serpent of Ch'ang Mountain.
Attack its head and its tail will strike; attack its tail and its head will strike.
Attack its middle and both head and tail will strike.
Venture to ask: "Can a strategy act the same as the *shuai jan*?"
I say: "It can. The men of Wu and the men of Yueh are rivals,
Yet if they were sailing in a ship that encountered a gale,
They would rescue one another just as the right hand assists the left."

Hence, it is not enough to rely on teamed horses and waiting wheels.
In the Tao of Politics, courage comes from acting as One.
In the Management of Situations, both weak and strong must succeed.
Therefore, those skilled in the execution of Strategy
Lead the One, as if by hand, until there is nothing left to gain.

The Work of the Leaders of the Force
Is secrecy through silence and control through straightforwardness.
They are able to keep the eyes and ears of the team uninformed and unknowing;
They alter the Work and adjust the Plan so that others cannot discern;
They alter the position and detour the route so that others cannot calculate.

When the command initiates the deadline,
It is like climbing a ladder and losing one's footing.
When the command initiates a penetration,
The leader approaches the Situation and releases the arrow.
Burn the boat, break the cauldron, push here and there as if herding sheep,
And none will know the destination.
To assemble the Entire Force and all its numbers, and to thrust ahead formidably —
Such is the Work of the Leader of the Force.

The Chinese snake name *shuai jan* translates literally as "spontaneously responsive."
Chuan Chu and Ts'ao Kuei were military heroes of the Warring States era.

九地之變，屈伸之利，人情之理，不可不察也。

凡爲客之道，深則專，淺則散。

去國越境而師者，絕地也；四達者，衢地也；入深者，重地也；入淺者，輕地也；背固前險者，圍地也；無所往者，死地也。

是故散地吾將一其志；輕地吾將使之屬；爭地吾將趨其後；交地吾將謹其守；衢地吾將固其結；重地吾將繼其食；圯地吾將進其塗；圍地吾將塞其闕；死地吾將示之以不活。

故兵之情，圍則禦，不得已則鬬，過則從。

是故不知諸侯之謀者，不能預交；不知山林險阻沮澤之形者，不能行軍；不用鄉導者，不能得地利。

THE WAY OF THE ADVENTURER

The Nine Situations and Variations
Expand and manipulate the advantages and manage the condition of others.
Their study cannot be neglected.

Generally, it is the Tao of the Adventurer
To penetrate as a result of Focus and to be superficial as a result of Idleness.
Those who are in an Isolated Situation
Must cross over the boundaries of the organization toward the opposition.
Those who are in an Intersecting Situation
Must communicate all around.
Those who are in a Serious Situation
Must penetrate deeply.
Those who are in a Simple Situation
Must penetrate superficially.
Those who are in a Surrounded Situation
Must defend the exit and narrow the advance.
Those who are in a Desperate Situation
Must press onward without a location.

Thus, in Idle Situations, we lead by directing ourselves as One.
In Simple Situations, we lead by making use of dependent domains.
In Competitive Situations, we lead by hurrying our backups.
In Negotiable Situations, we lead by attending to our defenses.
In Intersecting Situations, we lead by strengthening our connections.
In Serious Situations, we lead by maintaining the flow of provisions.
In Obstructed Situations, we lead by advancing on the Path.
In Surrounded Situations, we lead by blocking any openings.
In Desperate Situations, we lead by making it known we may not survive.

For under the conditions of Strategy,
Those who are surrounded will resist;
Those who can neither gain nor stop will fight;
Those who are beyond their limit will obey.

Therefore, those who do not know the Plan of other leaders
Are not prepared to negotiate.
Those who do not know the positions of the mountains, forests, passes, and marshes
Are not able to Move the Force.
Those who do not employ local guides
Are not able to gain advantage in the Situation.

四五者，不知一，非霸王之兵也。

夫霸王之兵，伐大國，則其眾不得聚；威加於敵，則其交不得合。

是故不爭天下之交，不養天下之權，信己之私，威加於敵，故其城可拔，其國可墮。

施無法之賞，懸無政之令，犯三軍之眾，若使一人。

犯之以事，勿告以言；犯之以利，勿告以害。

投之亡地然後存，陷之死地然後生。夫眾陷於害，然後能為勝敗。

故為兵之勢，在於順佯敵之意，并敵一向，千里殺將，此謂巧能成事者也。

是故政舉之日，夷關拆符，無通其使。厲於廊廟之上，以誅其事。

敵人開闔，必亟入之。先其所愛，微與之期；踐墨隨敵，以決戰事。

是故始如處女，敵人開戶；後如脫兔，敵不及拒。

THE STRATEGY OF THE SUPERIOR LEADER

Those who do not know every one of the Nine
Cannot Strategize as does a Superior Leader.

The Strategy of the Superior Leader
Is to thwart a large organization so that their numbers cannot grow;
And to inspire awe among their opponents so that their meetings do not unify.

Therefore, they do not meet to compete with the Entire System.
They do not cultivate their authority over the Entire System.
They trust in themselves to inspire awe among their opponents.
In this way they uproot fortifications and overcome organizations.

Grant rewards without regard to Principles.
Issue commands without regard to Politics.
Wield the Entire Force and its numbers as if One.
Wield them to achieve the Work — never discuss it in speeches.
Wield them to achieve the advantages — never discuss the disadvantages.

Then, thrust into a perilous Situation, they will survive.
Then, trapped in a desperate Situation, they will live.
For it is when the numerous are trapped in disadvantage
That they are able to triumph over defeat.

Hence, to make a Strategy Work,
Consistently feign acceptance of the opponent's objectives,
Then turn on the opponent as One.
Even from a thousand miles away the command can be destroyed.
This is what is meant by the Work that ingenuity can accomplish.

Thus, the day that the policy is initiated,
Close off the outside and void the passes;
Do not send messages with envoys;
Rouse those at headquarters to execute the Work.

When opponents open a doorway, swiftly penetrate it.
Locate beforehand their deepest attachments, then inspire subtle expectations.
Follow the rules and accommodate the opponent,
All the while Working toward the decisive challenge.

Hence, appear at first as an innocent until the opponent opens the door.
Then, act in a flash so the opponent is unable to resist.

The word *nine* comes from the first two ideograms of this passage,
which translate as "four" and "five" respectively.

CHAPTER TWELVE

THE
FIERY ATTACK

(THE DECISIVE THRUST)

SUN TZU BELIEVED THAT OPEN CONFRONTATION WAS INEVI-
tably destructive and must be viewed only as a tactic of last resort. *The Art
of Strategy* was written as a guide to achieving objectives through strategic
maneuvering, and not through battle. Of course, open confrontation may
occur during a conflict, but it has no real place in a sophisticated strategy.
Sun Tzu said: "An intense View is not a reason to launch an opposition. An
angry leader is not a reason to initiate a challenge.... Intensity can cycle
back to fondness. Anger can cycle back to satisfaction. But an extinct
organization cannot cycle back to survival. And those who are destroyed
cannot cycle back to life."

Should open confrontation erupt, Sun Tzu insisted that it is vital and
humane to conclude it very quickly. The Fiery Attack is Sun Tzu's strategy
for delivering the decisive thrust — a maneuver designed to overwhelm the
opponent and end the conflict rapidly. He described five ways to create a
such a crisis and called these maneuvers Fire in the group, Fire in the supplies, Fire in transportation or communication, Fire in the treasury, and Fire
in the procedures. He explained, "Those who challenge to win and Attack
to take control, and yet do not study these effects, are destined to the misfortune known as Wasteful Delay."

CONFLICT IN THE SELF   A conflict with an inner opponent is
quite often an equally matched encounter, so it is possible that careful positioning and tactical maneuvering may not lead to a lasting victory. Sun Tzu
used the example of water to describe these subtler strategies. He said:
"Those whose Attack is reinforced with water must be strong, since water
can isolate but cannot overcome."

If you have not yet outmaneuvered your inner opponent, then bring your
struggle out into the open in order to execute the decisive thrust. Sun Tzu
said: "If a Fire can be started on the outside, do not wait for a time to start it
on the inside." Support from the outside — from experienced individuals
or special-interest organizations — will help you start the Fire that can overwhelm your inner opponent.

Concentrate now on working quickly, and do not prolong the confrontation. Delay during direct confrontation will tap your strength and
undermine your determination. Enlist help from the outside and make every
action count.

CONFLICT IN THE ENVIRONMENT   A direct confrontation with
an environment is very risky for the individual. Overcoming an environmental conflict through open confrontation is a form of revolution because it
is based on ultimatum and not on negotiation. The timing for such an
encounter must be exact, and, in order to protect yourself, your strategy

must include an alternative environmental destination.

Should an open confrontation erupt in your environment, you must move quickly. To achieve a meaningful lasting environmental objective you must force sweeping changes into the system, and they must occur rapidly and in direct response to your strategy. Sun Tzu would call this Starting a Fire.

After you have unleashed your strategy and ignited your environment, be on guard for a possible change of plans. Sun Tzu said: "If a Fire has exhausted its strength, pursue if there is opportunity; stop if there is not." If you cannot bring the changes you need to your relationship with your environment, you must execute a decisive thrust to propel you elsewhere — to another environment where you can find what you require for your growth and happiness.

CONFLICT WITH ANOTHER   If you are suddenly engaged in an open confrontation, then your strategy of tactical positioning and objective detachment has failed, and you have not been able to restructure or transcend your relationship. This happens when you and your opponent are evenly matched in strength, while your points of view are in complete discord.

A direct confrontation with another is an encounter of great intensity. Ordinarily, open confrontations conclude quickly since they cannot be maintained for long. Therefore, during confrontation you can triumph only through decisive and ultimate actions. Take the initiative and start the Fire that will determine the outcome.

Choose an area where your opponent is vulnerable to force a final confrontation — a Fiery Attack. Ignite the situation to absorb your opponent's energy and attention. Then Attack the relationship in its entirety to conclude it. "If a Fire is started on the inside," Sun Tzu instructed, "respond at once from the outside." Be on guard, however. Do not act if your opponent does not react, for you may not have delivered a decisive blow. Sun Tzu pointed out: "If a Fire is started and the strategy is silence, hold back and do not Attack."

CONFLICT AMONG LEADERS   In life, the first principle of survival is that the overall system must be preserved. Since open confrontation endangers that system, Sun Tzu called for prudence in leadership. When rivals face each other, he warned: "Do not move unless it is advantageous. Do not execute unless it is effective. Do not challenge unless it is critical."

Should open confrontation erupt between rival organizations, it is a leader's primary tactical responsibility to strike the decisive blow as quickly as possible — to overwhelm the rival with a preemptive display of power or numbers. Sun Tzu believed that the ability to bring confrontation to a timely conclusion is the mark of enlightened and humane leadership. Without decisive action the struggle will be prolonged, a situation Sun Tzu called Wasteful Delay.

Confrontation must come about only as a last resort and can be viewed only as a failure in negotiation strategy. The Fiery Attack is Sun Tzu's guide to ending a destructive encounter rapidly and favorably. To execute a Fiery Attack, a superior leader creates a crisis in the opponent's support system. This distracts the opponent, which in turn provides the opportunity for triumph.

孫子曰：

凡火攻有五：一曰火人，二曰火積，三曰火輜，四曰火庫，五曰火隊。

行火必有因，烟火必素具。

發火有時，起火有日。

時者，天之燥也；日者，宿在箕、壁、翼、軫也。

凡此四宿者，風起之日也。

THE FIVE FIERY ATTACKS

Sun Tzu said:

Generally, there are Five Fiery Attacks.
The first is Fire in the group.
The second is Fire in the supplies.
The third is Fire in the transport.
The fourth is Fire in the treasury.
The fifth is Fire in the procedures.

A moving Fire will show the way;
A signal Fire will make preparations clear.

There are seasons to start Fires;
There are days to start Fires.
The season is when the weather is dry;
The day depends on the constellations
Of the Sieve, the Wall, the Wings, and the Chariot.
Generally, these four constellations mark the days of the rising wind.

"The days of the rising wind" follow the nights the moon moves in the constellations of
Sagittarius (the Sieve), Pegasus (the Wall), Craterus (the Wings), or Corvus (the Chariot [Platform]).
These are four of the twenty-eight constellations that divided the night sky for early Chinese astronomers.
It takes approximately twenty-eight days, or a lunar month, for the moon to travel through all of them.

凡火攻，必因五火之變而應之。

火發於內，則早應之於外。

火發而其兵靜者，待而勿攻。

極其火力，可從而從之；不可從而止。

火可發於外，無待於內，以時發之。

火發上風，無攻下風。晝風久；夜風止。

凡軍必知有五火之變，以數守之。

THE FIVE FIERY VARIATIONS

Generally, in a Fiery Attack,
There are Five Fiery Variations
That must be followed and responded to.

If a Fire is started on the inside,
Respond at once from the outside.

If a Fire is started and the Strategy is silence,
Hold back and do not Attack.

If a Fire has exhausted its strength,
Pursue if there is opportunity;
Stop if there is not.

If a Fire can be started on the outside,
Do not wait for a time to start it on the inside.

If a Fire starts upwind,
Do not Attack from downwind.
In the daytime the wind may last;
At night the wind may stop.

Generally, the Force must understand the Five Fiery Variations
In order to analyze its own defense.

故以火佐攻者明。

以水佐攻者強。水可以絕，
不可以奪。

夫戰勝攻取，而不修其功者凶，
命曰費留。

故曰：
明主慮之，良將修之。

THE DECISIVE TECHNIQUES

Those whose Attack is reinforced with Fire are enlightened.

Those whose Attack is reinforced with water must be strong,
Since water can isolate but cannot overcome.

Those who challenge to win
And Attack to take control,
And yet do not study these effects,
Are destined to the misfortune known as Wasteful Delay.

Therefore it is said:
"A Brilliant View is calculated;
Good Leadership is cultivated."

非利不動，非得不用，非危不戰。

主不可以怒而興師，將不可以慍而致戰。

合於利而動，不合於利而止。

怒可以復喜，慍可以復悅，亡國不可以復存，死者不可以復生。

故明君慎之，良將警之。

此安國全軍之道也。

THE ULTIMATE RESTRAINT

Do not move unless it is advantageous.
Do not execute unless it is effective.
Do not challenge unless it is critical.

An intense View is not a reason to launch an opposition.
An angry leader is not a reason to initiate a challenge.

If engagement brings advantage, move.
If not, stop.

Intensity can cycle back to fondness.
Anger can cycle back to satisfaction.
But an extinct organization cannot cycle back to survival.
And those who are destroyed cannot cycle back to life.

Thus, a Brilliant Ruler is prudent;
A Good Leader is on guard.

Such is the Tao of a Stable Organization and a Complete Force.

CHAPTER THIRTEEN

THE USE OF INTELLIGENCE

(THE INFORMATION ADVANTAGE)

SUN TZU CONCLUDES *THE ART OF STRATEGY* WITH HIS MOST HU-mane chapter. Here he describes the Use of Intelligence-gathering techniques to curb costly mistakes and human suffering. Fighting and strife — in oneself, in the home, in a relationship, or among groups — is without doubt the most destructive force in nature. However justifiable the battle may appear, it can nevertheless destroy life, unity, and resources, while damaging the entire system. Sun Tzu said of open conflict: "A thousand pieces of gold will be spent each day. On the inside and the outside there will be upheaval. The work and the property of seven hundred thousand will be disrupted and mutual defenses will be maintained for years, just to compete for one day of triumph."

Sun Tzu believed that the greatest rewards and most generous support should go to those who are employed to gather information. He described five types of information-gathering: Local Intelligence is information from those in the vicinity; Inside Intelligence is information from those within the opponent's circle; Counterintelligence is information from an opponent's agent; Deadly Intelligence is misinformation supplied to an opponent's agent; and Secure Intelligence is published misinformation that disorders an opponent's priorities. Sun Tzu stated that a brilliant leader will Use and coordinate all of these Intelligences. He said: "This is called the Divine Web. It is the treasure of the Ruler."

CONFLICT IN THE SELF   It is time once again for reflection. Your greatest obstacle in your struggle to overcome an inner conflict is a lack of information about your opponent. *The Art of Strategy* ends here by cycling back to its first chapter, "The Calculations," where you are instructed to examine yourself and the problem you wish to terminate.

When confronting bad habits, character weaknesses, psychological blocks to achievement, or self-destructive patterns of conduct, you must first discover how and why this conflict is at work in your life. Is there a part of yourself fulfilled or protected by your inner opponent? Somewhere in your personality your inner opponent is finding the support it needs to continue.

Find that part of yourself that supports your inner opponent. Fear of the unknown or fear of failure will block motivation. A sense of emotional well-being that is based on physical indulgence is an association that creates crippling behavior disorders. Wrongful childhood programming that has resulted in feelings of inferiority or worthlessness is the feeding ground for an inner opponent. Work for clarity; it will lead you to triumph.

CONFLICT IN THE ENVIRONMENT   A well-planned and skillfully executed Intelligence-gathering strategy is vital to the success of an environmental challenge. It is essential to know what drives the mechanism that surrounds you — and to know just where it is being driven. Sun Tzu said: "If the objective is to attack a Fortified Area, leaders must defend themselves with Foreknowledge of supporters, advisors, guardians, and influencers."

An environment is a collaborative structure. Many others have participated in its cultivation and at least one ideology has been satisified by its existence. Thus, as an individual unfulfilled by your environment, your choices are limited: You can reposition yourself more advantageously by increasing your contribution to this closed system politically, financially, or socially; you can restructure your environment through persuasion or revolution; or you can move yourself to a more suitable and receptive situation.

Inform yourself about every aspect of your environment. Make certain that the existence of your conflict does not directly benefit your environment — that you are not a pawn in a larger game — for if that is the case, you have no choice but flight. Base your strategy on awareness and carefully gathered Intelligence and you will have your destiny firmly under control.

CONFLICT WITH ANOTHER   It is the nature of humans to adjust to one another by selectively ignoring personality clashes. Many intimate relationships run smoothly this way and, over time, turning a blind eye to problems becomes an art. Although you may be unpracticed in the close and objective examination of your opponent, it is now the key to your triumph.

Locate the information you need, regardless of the cost. Consult with others, ask questions, seek insights. Especially, obtain Intelligence about your opponent's past experiences and future hopes. Make certain that you are examining the relationship in its entirety and are prepared to confront it completely.

As you plan your strategy, gather your information confidentially, and prepare to apply it spontaneously. Sun Tzu pointed out that "intelligence cannot be employed without enlightenment and intuition.... The Work of Intelligence cannot succeed without subtlety and ingeniousness."

CONFLICT AMONG LEADERS   Perhaps more so than any other defensive strategy, Intelligence-gathering is critical to the successful outcome of interorganizational conflicts. With advance information, costly mistakes can be avoided, destruction averted, and the path to lasting triumph made clear. For this reason, Sun Tzu believed that "Nothing should be as favorably regarded as Intelligence; nothing should be as generously rewarded as Intelligence."

In interorganizational struggles, effective negotiations and productive victories are entirely dependent on fact-finding and discovery. Surprise is the real enemy during confrontation. Therefore, superior strategists take care to uncover their opponent's secrets and "hidden agendas," while maintaining their own security.

Of the five kinds of Intelligence that Sun Tzu described, good leaders are especially skilled in Counterintelligence, or the Use of agents from rival organizations. Through Counterintelligence, strategic misinformation can flow out of the organization and into the opponent's circle — information designed to reposition the opposition for defeat. "Subtly, very subtly," Sun Tzu exclaimed, "nowhere neglect the Use of Intelligence."

孫子曰：

凡興師十萬，出兵千里，百姓之費，公家之奉，

日費千金。內外騷動，怠於道路，不得操事者，七十萬家。

相守數年，以爭一日之勝。

而愛爵祿百金，不知敵之情者，不仁之至也，

非人之將也，非主之佐也，非勝之主也。

故明君賢將，所以動而勝人，成功出於眾者，先知也。

先知者，不可取於鬼神，不可象於事，不可驗於度，

必取於人，知敵之情者也。

OBTAINING FOREKNOWLEDGE

Sun Tzu said:

Generally, raising a corps of a hundred thousand
And covering a thousand miles to put forth a Strategy
Will consume the income of the People and the property of the Public.

A thousand pieces of gold will be spent each day.
On the inside and the outside there will be upheaval.
On the path of the Tao there will be negligence.
The work and property of seven hundred thousand will be disrupted
And mutual defenses will be maintained for years,
Just to compete for one day of triumph.

Those who do not have knowledge of the opponent's condition
Because they begrudge a hundred pieces of gold or an official promotion
Are the cause of inhumanity.
They do not have Leadership and do not reinforce the View.
So the View cannot triumph.

Thus, it is Foreknowledge that enables
A Brilliant Ruler and an Excellent Leader
To triumph over others wherever they move,
While producing useful achievements for the numerous.

Foreknowledge cannot be obtained through spirits or the supernatural.
It cannot be projected though Effort.
It cannot be verified through measurements.

Those who have knowledge of the opponent's condition
Are certain to obtain it through others.

故用間有五：有因間，有內間，有反間，有死間，有生間。

五間俱起，莫知其道，是謂神紀，人君之寶也。

因間者，因其鄉人而用之。

內間者，因其官人而用之。

反間者，因其敵間而用之。

死間者，為誑事於外，令吾間知之，而傳於敵。

生間者，反報也。

故三軍之親，莫親於間，賞莫厚於間，事莫密於間。

非聖智不能用間，非仁義不能使間，非微妙不能得間之實。

微哉微哉，無所不用間也。

間事未發而先聞者，間與所告者皆死。

THE DIVINE WEB

There are Five Uses of Intelligence:
There is Local Intelligence;
There is Inside Intelligence;
There is Counterintelligence;
There is Deadly Intelligence;
There is Secure Intelligence.

When the Five Intelligences all occur together
And none know of the method,
This is called the Divine Web.
It is the treasure of the Ruler.

Local Intelligence is Using natives to show the way.

Inside Intelligence is Using others' officials to show the way.

Counterintelligence is Using the opponent's Intelligence to show the way.

Deadly Intelligence is Working to deceive outwardly.
We knowingly direct the Intelligence and pass it on to the opponent.

Secure Intelligence is falsifying reports.

Hence, in the Work of the Entire Force,
Nothing should be as favorably regarded as Intelligence;
Nothing should be as generously rewarded as Intelligence;
Nothing should be as confidential as the Work of Intelligence.

Intelligence cannot be employed without enlightenment and intuition.
Intelligence cannot be used without humanity and generosity.
The Work of Intelligence cannot succeed without subtlety and ingeniousness.

Subtly, very subtly,
Nowhere neglect the Use of Intelligence.

But if the Work of Intelligence has not yet begun,
Then those who discuss it beforehand, and those who listen,
Are both dangerous.

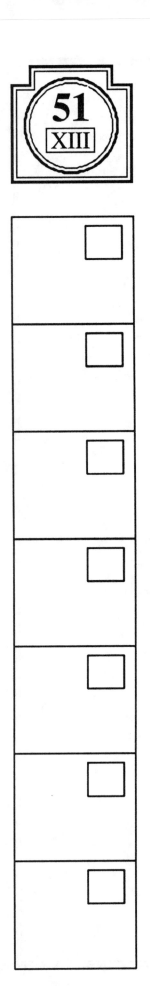

凡軍之所欲擊，城之所欲攻，人之所欲殺，必先知其守將，左右，謁者，門者，舍人之姓名，令吾間必索知之。

必索敵人之間來間我者，因而利之，導而舍之，故反間可得而用也。

因是而知之，故鄉間內間，可得而使也。

因是而知之，故死間爲誑事，可使告敵。

因是而知之，牧生間可使如期。

五間之事，主必知之，知之必在反間，故反間不可不厚也。

THE IMPORTANCE OF COUNTERINTELLIGENCE

Generally, if the objective is to attack a corps,
Or if the objective is to attack a Fortified Area,
Or if the objective is to destroy another,
Leaders must defend themselves with Foreknowledge
Of supporters, advisors, guardians, and influencers.
We must direct our Intelligence to examine this knowledge.

Our Intelligence must examine our opponents
By approaching their Intelligence,
Showing the way to advantages,
Leading the way to shelter.
In this way, Counterintelligence is obtained and employed.

Counterintelligence will show the way to further knowledge
By obtaining and using Local Intelligence and Inside Intelligence.

Counterintelligence will show the way to further knowledge
By Working with Deadly Intelligence to send deceptive information to the opponent.

Counterintelligence will show the way to further knowledge
By using Secure Intelligence to create deadlines.

The View must be made aware of the Work of the Five Intelligences.
Certain knowledge depends on Counterintelligence.
Therefore, Counterintelligence must be treated with full generosity.

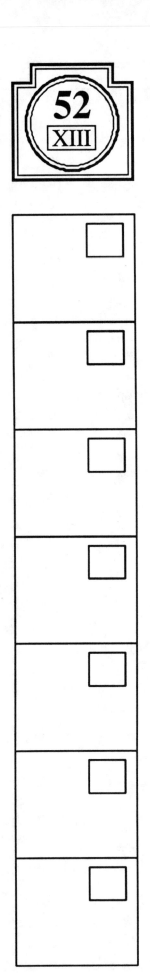

昔殷之興也，伊摯在夏；周之興也，呂牙在殷。

故惟明君賢將，能以上智爲間者，必成大功。

三軍之所恃而動也。

此兵之要。

THE ESSENCE OF STRATEGY

In Ancient Times,
The rise of the Yin Dynasty
Was due to I Chih of the Hsia Dynasty;
And the rise of the Chou Dynasty
Was due to Lu Ya of the Yin Dynasty.

Hence, only a Brilliant Ruler and an Excellent Leader,
Who are able to conduct their Intelligence with superiority and cleverness,
Are certain to achieve great results.
The Entire Force relies on this for every move.

This is the Essence of Strategy.

I Chih was an official of the Hsia Dynasty (c 2000 to c 1520 B.C.)
who acted as an agent for the Yin Dynasty (the latter part of the Shang Dynasty (c 1520 to c 1030 B.C.).

Lu Ya was an official of the Yin Dynasty
who acted as an agent for the Chou Dynasty (c 1030 to 207 B.C.).